CHRISM

OF

THE

CHILD

VINCENTE GARCIA

CHRISM OF THE CHILD

A MEMOIR

VINCENTE GARCIA

Author of Inspiration for Your Eternal Life:
Fifteen Ways To Be Saved

Copyright © 2025 Vincente Garcia

All rights reserved. No portion of this book may be reproduced in any form without written permission from the publisher or author, except as permitted by U.S. copyright law, except for the use of brief quotations in a book review.

ISBN 978-1-954736-37-5 (Paperback)

Library of Congress Control Number: 2025951011

Authors Inside
P.O. Box 221
Nipomo, CA 93444
www.authorsinside.org

Cover design: *Laura Gaisie*

Editor: *Patrick Ashman*

Printed in the United States of America

Contents

Chapter 1	The Whisper	1
Chapter 2	Faith for Self-Control	9
Chapter 3	The Divine Proof	17
Chapter 4	Compelled to Praise	23
Chapter 5	Mystery of the Lion	27
Chapter 6	Searching Spirit Knowledge	45
Chapter 7	Tangible Evidence	53
Chapter 8	The Realms	61
Chapter 9	Commitment	69
Chapter 10	The Enlightening	75
Chapter 11	Knowing What	85
Chapter 12	The Inspiration	91
Chapter 13	Knowing When	97
Chapter 14	Clearing the Path	111
Chapter 15	Seeking the Lost	143
Chapter 16	Little Miracles	157
Chapter 17	Foreknowledge	169
Chapter 18	The Image of Creation	201
Chapter 19	From God	225
Chapter 20	To God	237
	About the Author	255

Chapter 1 - The Whisper

I am created, and I am created me in Spirit. And just like everyone else who was ever created in Spirit into flesh for this Earthly Realm, I must learn to understand why I am recreated me in Spirit for the Heavenly Realm.

Growing up as a child around the age of five, I did not know the difference between right and wrong yet. As I was seeing things for the first time with all the curiosity of a child wanting to know why things were created the way they are, my mind was exploring and looking for the boundaries of the things hidden from me while I was simply existing in this world.

On a hot sunny day, while I was playing outside in the grass and running through the sprinklers in the grass to cool off, I ran across a wet sidewalk with bare feet and slipped, falling hard onto my back side. I bruised the back of my head on the sidewalk. The pain from the impact was excruciating, so I started to cry while I ran into the house to get help from my mother. I looked, but I could not find her in the house, so I felt alone with no one to help me ease my pain as it got worse. I laid my body face down on her bed and closed my tearful eyes as I wished for the hurt to stop.

As I was crying with my eyes closed, I began to see my thoughts: that I was alive and living inside my body and my body was not really me. I could feel my existence within my body, and I wanted to believe that it was separate from me. I did not want to believe that I was hurt anymore, and only the body I was in was injured and hurting, I just did not know how to make it stop.

Suddenly, I heard a whisper inside me, and it said to me, "Get up! You are going to be okay." That's when I first believed that I was inside my body, and that something good was speaking within me with a voice of authority that distracted me from dwelling on the pain. For some reason, that brought me comfort. At that moment, I became aware that something new to me was part of my existence. And I knew in my mind that it was with me wherever I went. From the time I walked away from the bed, I could feel its presence.

I touched the bruise on the back of my head and remembered that it was not me, it was the body that I was in, and it was all around me. I only had to wait for it to get better, and I was okay with that because I then believed I wasn't hurt, I was safe inside my body. From that time on, that is how I knew myself. I thought that everyone else must also view themselves in the same way and that I was just finding out about the voice that taught me it was with me, and that I wasn't alone anymore. Somehow, I was assured by the tone of the voice that it was watching out for me in a way that let me know I would grow up to be safe and that it would never steer me wrong.

THE WHISPER

A couple of years later, around the age of seven, just before the winter holidays, my mother asked me what I wanted for Christmas and without hesitation I had a picture pop into my mind of what I wanted. I wanted a toy truck that I could load things into the back part of it. I had no idea why I asked for that; the words just came out of my mouth like someone else said it through me. Nevertheless, for Christmas she got me a toy truck that had little compartments on the back of it that came with little plastic animal figurines to put in each of them. My favorite figurine was the lion; it was the most life-like figure to me.

In those days, my family never owned a television, and I never watched one. I would play with the toy truck and animals on the living room rug next to our console radio as I was listening closely to the words of the singers' voices coming out of the speaker. I wondered how that was made possible. I would put my ear close up to the speaker and close my eyes to listen intently for the changing sounds of their voices. I wanted to hear them more clearly because I thought it gave the words in the songs more feeling that they were projecting in harmony with the music. I was amazed that I could hear a person speaking from another place, and that they didn't have to be in the same room for me to know that the sounds had to come from a living person.

One day, when my mother and father were at work and I was alone in our apartment, I was laying on the living

VINCENTE GARCIA

room rug on my belly playing with my toy truck and animals. The console radio was playing my favorite songs, so I started listening to the voices coming from the speaker with my ear up close to it and with my eyes closed for a while, when I was surprised to hear the voice of someone who was calling me from the dining room behind me. Since I was startled, I turned my body and my head quickly to look in the direction of the voice and opened my eyes. I was looking directly at the eyes of the Sacred Heart Tapestry of Jesus that was hanging on the wall next to the dining room table.

I knew that I was alone in the apartment, and I wondered, how did that just happen? I got up and walked over to the tapestry and remembered that I was told it was a picture of someone called Jesus who was a real Holy person that people prayed to. In the tapestry, Jesus had His left hand touching His heart and the other hand making what I learned was called a peace sign. I never for a second thought that the tapestry was alive. I was thinking that maybe Jesus was alive and speaking to me from somewhere else invisible to my eyesight. And since I could hear His voice inside and outside of me, I could pay attention in the direction He wanted me to look. I got the feeling He was teaching me something new that He can do for me to show me the specific things He wants me to learn.

So, I stared at the eyes of the tapestry while I posed with the same hand positions with my hands, and in my mind thought of the question, can you hear me? After a few seconds of standing very still while waiting and listening for His voice, I felt and heard simultaneously that the answer was, "Yes, I can hear you." That is how I knew it was really happening, because the feelings and the words happened as one whole thing at the same time. Then I felt a deep sense of closure when I remembered that I always wanted to know who was talking within me and bringing me internal peace since I was five.

Every so often, I would walk past the dining table, and I would hear my name being called in a way like I was being acknowledged with a hello at the same time from the direction of the tapestry. I would glance at it and think to myself and respond in my mind, "Hi, Jesus." And that was it: acknowledging Him was the appropriate thing to do and I didn't feel the need to tell anyone else about it because they really didn't comment much about it the first time I told them what had happened. Now, everything I did was ordinarily between myself and Him.

I knew Jesus Christ was real, alive, speaking, hearing, and teaching me. That was how I started to know Him. I noticed when He called me that He did not need to pronounce every syllable of every word as we speak with our mouths to explain everything. He would only need to speak like one sound to call me. Then, as I would listen intently, I would know what He was telling me and understand everything like He could pour all the words and meanings into my mind where I could feel it in my heart and never forget it. And He would remind me every so often that He was still with me, and that He always loved me very much because He wanted me to remember that He was always there for me. I could feel in my heart that the message was sincere.

I remembered His voice from the first time He spoke to me when I was five years old and learned that someone good could talk to me: the me that was living inside my body. And Jesus was the voice that was teaching me things, spiritual things that weren't being taught and explained to me by people. It was Jesus who taught me that the picture of the tapestry was what He looked like, and He confirmed that it is true, His Name is Jesus. I certainly couldn't learn that from a television or a video phone. Video phones weren't invented yet, and I didn't know anyone who owned a television. We didn't even own a black and white television yet in those days. We only used a console radio for music entertainment.

I would go on doing whatever came naturally to me when I was speaking and learning from the voice of Jesus. And it never crossed my mind at that time that I was on a serious spiritual path to know Him the way He wants true believers in Him to know Him. I was just a child having fun playing with other children and being as good as I could to everyone with a secret that no one believed anyway.

I lived to think the whispers that I could hear from Jesus were normally spoken to everyone for everyone else to hear and speak to Him too, since they would tell me they knew who Jesus was. I just didn't understand why no one liked to talk about Jesus openly without hesitation or why they would keep their answers brief if I asked questions. Like, as if it might be too complicated to explain everything they knew about Jesus to a seven-year-old kid who was claiming to hear the voice of Jesus talking to him.

So, eventually I stopped bothering people about what I was experiencing and kept it to myself because it made people feel uncomfortable. I didn't like that it would make my friends quiet, and I felt responsible for making them feel that way. It was somewhat sad for me to see them struggling for the answers anyway, and I didn't want to make them feel that way anymore. I had to learn to deal with it myself until I could learn the answers another way. So, I began to wait patiently and listen for the whispers of Jesus to talk to me again and maybe He would show me and teach me what the truth is, about who He is, and why He speaks to me in whispers.

Chapter 2 - Faith for Self-Control

Later that year, I found myself in bed with a high fever. It was the kind that made me weak and sensitive to sound. As I lay in bed, I could hear my own heartbeat pounding in my ears, like the heartbeats from an ultrasound except I could hear it in my eardrums and echoing in my mind, becoming louder the more I listened to it. It wasn't so bad at first, but after a day it became annoying. I closed my eyes and thought, if I ignore it, maybe it will go away, but that didn't work. Then I began to embrace the sound and concentrate on the pounding rhythm in my mind, thinking that it was just my body healing the fever in it. I would listen to my heartbeat until it became a comforting sound that I thought, if I focused my mind on it, would distract me from feeling sick until I could fall asleep and rest.

I was awakened in the night by a disturbing presence when I felt like I wasn't alone in my dark bedroom. The light of the moon faintly beamed through the window onto the floor between my bed and the other side of the dark room. I focused my eyes intently on the darkest part of the room, trying to make out the form of what darkness was there. Then I noticed something moving in the form of a large person which was like a statue of a man that was a spirit of complete darkness with no face. I saw its arms and legs moving around as it pushed itself up to stand from the sitting position where it was. Then I could see that it was the same pitch black in its entire form that was darker than the darkness in the room, but I couldn't tell what it was sitting on. I refused to engage in any way with it as I watched the silhouette of the dark man taking slow steps toward me. It became uncomfortable to look at it, so I closed my eyes and listened for any sound it could make as it was moving closer, but there was no sound. After a moment I looked around the room and felt like it was gone. Of course, I was relieved that it was gone, but I was curious if it would come back. I wondered, if I peered into the darkness again, whether it would reappear. So, I repeated the same thing, and after a little while, it reappeared, moving around a little differently each time. I was a little less frightened to know that if I did not focus on that evil thing to come out of the darkness it wouldn't. The question in my mind was, Why is it when I was looking at that ugly dark thing I would feel so nervous?

The next night I was still weak and tried to get some rest to get better, but I was restless. As I laid on my bed, I felt the weight of my body begin to press hard into the mattress. My eyes were closed, but I was still awake in my mind and body to understand what was happening to me. Then I felt as if the bed was floating up from the floor with me in it, which wasn't so bad until it started to tilt forward, and I felt my body wanting to slide off the bed. I resisted by remaining as still as possible and keeping the thought and feeling of the pressure of my body on the mattress. Then it tilted back to the flat position and started to tilt backwards with my feet up until I was hanging straight upside down as my back started to separate a little from the mattress until I started to feel like I could slide off the bed and fall head first onto the floor. I closed my eyes and continued to focus on the thought of not coming away from the mattress until my body became pressed into the mattress again. As soon as that happened, I felt the bed suddenly flip upside down until I was facing the floor. It became difficult to stay focused by the thought of remaining attached to the mattress, which was my only thought to keep myself from falling off the bed.

After a few seconds, I felt a sense of calm throughout my body as I was pressing lightly against the bed, so I opened my eyes and saw that the bed was moving through space in one direction and I wasn't facing down at all. Objects like shooting stars were flying past me from a far distance and there was nothing above or below -only the sight of myself attached to my bed moving and tumbling through space. I could feel the centrifugal force of my body spinning against and away from the mattress as my body was beginning to separate from the mattress. I didn't want to be there anymore with the thought of falling off the mattress and being lost in that place.

I closed my eyes again and laid as still as possible to calm my fears as I thought of being back in my bedroom. I could picture myself at a distance from my bedroom in space, then I somehow quickly returned back into my bedroom where I was laying on my bed from the beginning. When I felt that I had returned, I opened my eyes and saw that I was in my room. I began to wonder why all these things were happening to me; if it was that dark, evil thing torturing me in my sickness, then I knew that I needed to learn not to be afraid of anything and remain calm to control what was happening to me.

So, I closed my eyes again and focused my mind on going back to that place, where I instantly reappeared when I opened my eyes. This time I remained as calm as I could as I tumbled through space faster and faster until it wouldn't go any faster as I was able to remain attached to the mattress with all my might until I became fearless.

After a while, I felt like I could anticipate all the tumbling movements in advance, and it became easier to rationally sync my thoughts and emotions to everything that was happening, to understand how to control myself. When I focused my thoughts to see myself on the bed, I could see myself firmly attached to the bed from a short distance and the tumbling would stop so I could see that I was in control of my position. Once again, when I wanted to return to my bedroom I closed my eyes and focused my mind to think of going back to my bedroom by seeing it from a distance in

FAITH FOR SELF-CONTROL

space again. I waited until I felt perfectly still with the weight of my body flat on my bed before I opened my eyes to see that I was returned back to my bedroom where I started. I remembered what I had been through and thought that it was kind of fun tumbling through space, so I thought that I would go back one more time to be sure that I had no fear of tumbling through space.

That last time I noticed that I didn't need to remain attached to my bed anymore, which I was doing only because it was my wish to do that, and that I could control the tumbling and traveling through space if I remained calm and in control by focusing my mind on the position that I was in and the direction I wished to move toward. I no longer needed to see myself outside of my body to gain control, I could do it from within my body. My fear of being out of control was gone when I returned from that place.

I don't ever feel the need to go back there, because I had learned that my Spirit of self-control, which is stronger than my fear, comes from my having faith in my abilities without the fear of anything by keeping my mind focused and in control of myself no matter where I was or what I was doing. That is how I was taught to remain fearless of the unknown things that come out of the darkness which seemed to want to make me fear. I had to remember that Jesus was teaching me through my mind to never be afraid because He is with me and teaching me to live without fear in the Spirit Realm, which is infinite compared to the Earthly Realm of matter.

Learning to live in Spirit is the superior way of life by understanding that the Spirit controls the body and the mind. That is how my Lord Jesus Christ helps me learn in an instant what could take a person a lifetime. This is why it is essential to understand the visions and dreams that we are shown by asking the Holy Spirit to guide us to the interpretation and simple truth in their meanings.

I have been taught that dreams and visions are a way of bringing out my passion for every kind of situation that I will encounter in my life in advance, so that I may align the proper level of emotional reaction I must have for them with Spiritual self-control when they do happen. And understanding those kinds of things in advance makes me more Spiritually powerful to deal with problems by the Word of GOD, and less likely to fall into sin by confusion.

As a Chosen One, it is now vital for me to practice living by the Spirit to remember the lessons I have been taught by my Lord Jesus Christ from the various experiences He has put me through, so I will not falter at the time I recognize that a calamity is present. This is how I remain attached to my Lord Jesus Christ. I know when I turn to Him for answers that He will remind me of all my strength at once through the power of the Holy

FAITH FOR SELF-CONTROL

Spirit in me with the clarity in my mind from the Word of Truth that He put in my heart to remember. It is up to me to act by the truth that I know is in accord with the Word of Truth by living in the New Covenant of the Spirit of my Lord Jesus Christ. With His help, I am living with the power of GOD the Father through HIS Holy Spirit, without any fear or doubt in my faith for self-control.

Chapter 3 - The Divine Proof

For a few months, I lived knowing that Jesus was real in my life, and if He wanted to tell me something, I could understand Him by His voice while I was awake or see things in my dreams that He wanted me to know. That was how I carried on from day to day. But this was just the beginning of my Spiritual journey of understanding the realms I was experiencing.

Sometimes I would lay in bed at night trying to go to sleep like my mother told me to do. I would think of all the spiritual things that I experienced in my life, awake or in dreams. I understood some of it, yet there still remained some questions as to how things work between people and the spirits- most of all, why were they so active in my life?

I would tell my siblings I had a dream: that when I grow up I'm going to have a truck that was high up in the air and made with big tires like balloons that I could drive up and down curbs anytime I want, and the tires would not pop. And I asked, wouldn't that be fun? People did not drive personal vehicles on the street like that in those days. And still, anyone that I mentioned these kinds of things to would seem to enjoy hearing about my dreams and would laugh at the things I described, but they never seemed to really believe it like I did. That, to me, was perplexing because I was telling the truth, and no one would ever question what I said, nor tell me they had experienced anything remotely similar to what was happening to me. It appeared to me that they were denying that what I said happened. It was a waste of time to look for others that may understand the mysteries of my life. Regardless of people's reactions, I still wanted to have a better understanding about what was happening to me.

One night while laying in bed, some questions came to my mind, like what was the dark man all about? And why haven't I stopped feeling uneasy about the thought of it? It must have been a bad thing that was trying to get to me. I didn't really want to see it again; I just wanted to know why it didn't make contact with me, and why I was still feeling uneasy about it. I couldn't sleep that night from thinking about it. I would open my eyes, and look around the dark room wondering if the dark man would finish what it started. Hours must have gone by, and I was exhausted, but I remained ready, opening my eyes from time to time to see if the dark man would appear to show me its face. I resisted focusing on it again because I really didn't want to bring it to me.

I covered my eyes with the blankets and tried to fall asleep when I had a feeling that I was not alone in the room anymore. Only this time, I had absolutely no fear of anything inside or outside of my body because I could feel and see the light in me and in my room. I slowly brought the blanket away from my eyes and felt liberated in the highest sense of the word. It was like peace, calmness, love, truth, understanding, and every possible goodness all at the same time in one feeling. Since I felt better, I opened my eyes just a little bit because I could see the light on my eyelids. I didn't know where this light was coming from that made it possible for me to see my pillow, my blankets, and the walls across my room. This was not regular light like from a bulb, the sun, or the moon. This light was alive, and it seemed to be hugging me with the most beautiful feeling of love.

I opened my eyes as much as I could, looked toward the footboard of my bed, and saw two very tall Angels dressed in full seamless Robes Of Light. They were standing side by side at each corner of my bed footboard as they stood still facing away from me. Their thick Robes Of Light completely covered their body; their hands that were together in front of them were covered by their sleeves, and their hoods were up laying gently over the top of their heads keeping the sides of their faces hidden from my sight as they were both facing away from me in constant prayer.

I felt a vibration of peacefulness and the presence of life coming from the Light. So, I sat up and put my face close to the Robes to look intently into the light coming from their Robes of Light. I could see that the light inside of them was alive and moving while the thought of beauty filled my eyes and my mind as the Light was constantly moving and penetrating through and over the folds of their Robes. The Angels remained still as they allowed me to look upon the Robes of Light while they seemed to desire to remain in prayer, so I never uttered a word. I only felt that what they were praying was powerful, good, and for my protection from darkness.

As I looked around the room, there was just enough light from them to let me see that there was no darkness anywhere in the room—not even a shadow. I could see every corner, every wall, the ceiling, the floor, and the stars in the clear night sky outside of my window just above and to the left side of my head. I had no doubt that they were there for me, to give me comfort from darkness forever. I could do nothing but love them back with everything I had in me. Without saying a word out loud, they spoke to me in my mind, telling me that it was time for me to rest. So, I thanked them in my mind with all the gratitude I had, pulled up my blankets over my eyes, and laid my head down to sleep in the love and peace coming from them.

From that night forward, I knew that I was being protected by the Angels from Jesus against the darkness of evil spirits no matter what. They let me know that the darkness of evil cannot harm anyone being protected by the living Spirit of Light, so long as we resist and reject all evil things. And it was important for me to keep seeking the truth about the Spirit and to follow the instructions that came to my mind and heart and the truth would come my way to be revealed over time.

I knew that Jesus would answer my questions as long as I waited with the thoughts of them in my mind as I had them ready to ask all the time. I now have the truth: that Jesus is the most loving and protecting One in the world, and He is with me because I believe He is here for me. And no one could ever change my mind no matter what after He showed me the divine proof of His Living Spirit of Light that He put in the Robes of Light. I believe in Jesus and love Him with my entire existence. And I knew that I had to listen patiently again for the next whispers from His divinity, which I know will always come to me without a doubt, the way I believe in His wonderful power and love for me, who He had chosen to show the truth by His divine proof of the Living Spirit of Light.

Chapter 4 - Compelled to Praise

By the age of nine, making new friends around me was as good as life was going to get when my only responsibility was to do well in school and finish my chores to help keep things tidy around the house. That summer, my father had bought us boys new suits for us to take pictures in that we sent to our family across the United States. It felt good to dress up in a suit, and I wanted to wear it again. But picture time was over, and I did not know of any reason to dress up again. We never dressed up formally for anything else we did.

Then I saw myself in a vision going to church in a suit and worshiping GOD. That's when I got the courage to ask my father to let me know when it was Sunday morning, because I wanted to go to church wearing my suit. To my surprise, he agreed to let me go. I asked if anyone else wanted to go with me, but the answer was no and that didn't matter to me.

Sure enough, on that next Sunday morning, the suit was put on and I walked across town to any church that I could find open to praise my LORD, GOD the Father, for sending HIS Son my Lord, Jesus, to be with me. I enjoyed being there to pray and sing praise the LORD for my Lord in songs. I never did get to know anyone in the church, but that wasn't what I was there for; I went there to pray and sing praises to GOD in the Name of

VINCENTE GARCIA

HIS Son. When Mass was over, I would walk to the next nearest church that I could find and listen for people singing or talking inside. If so, I would walk in with my suit, and jump right into praying and singing praises to my GOD again as soon as I could get a song book in my hands.

I had no idea what the bible said; I didn't even have a bible. I only knew that one thing was true: Jesus Christ and His Angels are real and everything about Him and them is the Holy Spirit of Light and all goodness from GOD the Father. He talked to me, He showed me His Angels in Robes Of Light, and by all means I knew I was being protected by all of them.

It had never crossed my mind to be saved by going to church; I was there to give thanks and honor to GOD for Jesus and the Ones who protected me and loved me like no one else could ever do. I knew that His love is beyond the comprehension of all people because I felt His love inside me and all around me. It's not describable in words; His love as He gives can only be experienced by knowing Him. And no one in the world could ever convince me otherwise. When I walked in and out of those churches, I was doing exactly what pleased my GOD the Father by worshipping and singing praises in the Name of HIS Son, Jesus, because I was being compelled from the inside out to do that, and nothing else in the world mattered to me at those times.

If I ever heard anyone say or hint that they don't believe in GOD or that Jesus Christ is real, the first thing that came to my mind was this question: how could anyone want to be so ignorant and lie about the truth? How sad it was to know that there were people who have not experienced the love from the Holiness of GOD. I knew the truth, and I wished that I had a way to prove it to others, because telling people didn't work. I knew that, somehow, they would have to see it for themselves to accept it. No one can make someone believe it, they would have to find out for themselves. I tried all my life to prove it by telling people what I saw and learned, but that just isn't enough for people. I just had to find the answer of how to tell people the truth someday. So, I kept my faith to myself and moved on in search of a way to help people believe in the truth. I knew I still had a lot to learn myself, so I continued to wait for Jesus and His whispers of divinity. I didn't know any other way to learn the truth except through Him teaching me in the way that only He knows how to make me learn by living the experiences to understand about Him and to never forget. It's because I know Him, love Him, believe in Him, and trust Him that I am compelled to praise our GOD the Father in Spirit like He told me to do, before I ever read or owned a bible.

Chapter 5 - Mystery Of the Lion

It could not have been more than a year later by the age of ten, when I was gifted with another sacred vision that was set before my eyes while I was awake. At the time it happened, I was not made aware that it would take over fifty years for me to come to an understanding of its meaning or just how complicated it would be for me to learn it throughout my years living in the Spirit. As part of the revelation of its meaning, it was revealed to me in a way that I could explain the truth to others by the meanings of its message. Not only because some of the meanings were not in scriptures of the modern day bibles, but because I didn't have access to some of the books of knowledge that were not written in my own language, since they had not been interpreted and transcribed from the recently found ancient scrolls and made readily available for circulation until after the internet was made usable around the world.

Some of the things I had to find out were for the confirmation of the message and that the vision was, in fact, divinely revealed to me by my Lord Jesus Christ. I also learned from the translations of the Dead Sea scriptures and the Nag Hammadi scriptures, which had descriptions of things that were revealed to me as a Holy Child of GOD after I received the Chrism by my Lord Jesus Christ. Those scriptures have descriptions of things I saw in visions written in them that were never mentioned in any other books of scripture or teaching of the bible that I have ever read or heard about before. It's no surprise to me that we don't have them in the modern day bibles because those other ancient scriptures were more recently discovered and translated for learning and comparisons. Some of the questions that I needed to be answered were not exactly on the minds of the authors of the bible books or the people who decided to leave them out of the bible and hidden from the world. But they are important to me in this day and age to solve the mystery of what my Lord Jesus Christ was showing me, of what to do and say, living in the Spirit today with incorruptible faith.

These gifts came for me at the Chrism of the Child that I am recreated me in Spirit, when I first became aware of GOD and HIS power of the Living Light, in the Spirit of HIS Son Jesus Christ, at the time I accepted living in Complete Unity with Him without a hint of hesitation to become One within me. He brought these gifts of visions to fulfill the refinement of my Spirit to have the understanding of the Word of Truth that I have been made ready for the purpose of helping others understand the hidden answers to my questions. They are now revelations from the Spirit of Truth, the Holy Spirit, which explains how and why the Spirit of Life, my Lord Jesus Christ, lives within me since He gave me the Chrism of the Child.

My sibling brother, who was one year older than I, would walk with me to our elementary school about a mile and a half away from home. After school, we would spend time with the school kids at the nearby park where there was an outside covered amphitheater stage for musicians, a recreation equipment room for kids to play games in, and a beautiful gated rose garden that looked like a maze we could walk into and enjoy being surrounded by the beauty and scent of the different colored rose flowers. Every once in a while, we would go into the rose garden to see who could pick the most beautiful flower of them all to take home to share with the family. We would run around playing tag through the trees and bushes throughout the park until it started getting dark or cold before we would call it a day and walk home.

One day my brother and I, and a friend of his from school that joined us that day had lost track of time while we were playing tag through the trees and bushes in the park until after the sun went down. We never did that before, and we noticed for the first time that part of the park was really dark because of the shadows of the many large trees that blocked the streetlights that were on the outer perimeter of the park.

My brother and his friend, being the eldest, suggested that it would be fun if we could stay and play hide and seek in the dark for a while before we walked home. I thought about it and agreed that it would be fun to hunt each other down in a dark park. Of course, they wanted to hide first, and I would go first to have to find them. I had all the confidence that I would be able to find them right away because I knew that park area like the back of my hand, and I wasn't afraid of the dark at all. I couldn't wait for my turn to hide in the dark from them, so I was willing to go first to get the game started.

The rule was that I had to count to one hundred out loud while facing away from the rose garden and covering my eyes. So, I quickly looked around for the best tree to lean on at the edge of the dark area to start counting. That's when I noticed for the first time that the outdoor amphitheater stage area at the corner of the park had some lighting that lit up the inside of the stage and the grassy area in front of it where the audience would sit on folding chairs, which were at that time put away in stacks against the inside right wall of the amphitheater stage dome, whenever they were not in use.

I decided to do my count standing in the shadow of a big old tree that was positioned at the front left side of the stage on the outer perimeter of the grassy area. I stood in the shadow of the tree which was cast from the lights on the stage. I leaned my head forward into my left arm that was against the tree trunk and counted to one hundred out loud. When I finished counting, I pushed myself away from the tree trunk as I opened my eyes facing the stage on my right side and saw something moving on the stage that caught my attention. It was about five feet long and moving around like a king cobra snake at the front left edge of the stage. My eyes were a little blurry from leaning them into my arm during the count, but they were coming into focus fast. That's when I noticed that it wasn't a snake, it was the tail of a beautiful Spirit Lion that glowed like it was emitting light from its body that had a very slight golden tint over its entire form. I was amazed to see the light from it shining brighter than the lights on the stage. I looked intently into its light at the side of its body and could see through it to the chairs stacked up on the other side of it against the wall on the stage area. That's when I noticed the Spirit Lion facing away from my direction. Its head and paws were pointed away from me at an angle toward the center of the stage as it was scanning the area from the center of the grassy area to the right side of the stage. So, I couldn't see its eyes looking in my direction as I was standing perfectly still while watching it move its head and its tail around.

I can't imagine that I had been standing there observing the Lion for more than fifteen seconds when I was surprised to feel my brothers' left hand on my right shoulder as he asked me, "what are you doing?" I didn't let him move me because I wanted to keep my eyes on the Lion so I wouldn't lose sight of it. I could see my brother's face in my peripheral vision at my right shoulder when I moved my right arm up and pointed at the Lion as I told him, "look right there on the stage".

VINCENTE GARCIA

Just as soon as I pointed at the Lion, he looked at it and I could see his friend's face move forward to the right side of my brother's face so he could see what my brother and I were looking at. Then I saw his friend's face turn to look at it too when I said, "It's a Lion." We were all quiet and still for a couple of seconds as we focused on the Lion together at the same time.

After what seemed like two seconds had passed, I noticed my brothers' face looking to his right for his friend, and I could see in my peripheral vision that he was gone. I didn't move, and I kept my hand up pointing at the Lion for my brother to look at it again and we both looked at it together again for what seemed like another couple of seconds. Then I slowly put my arm down, and thought to ask my brother what he wanted to do when I noticed he was gone too, and I was standing there alone in the park with the Spirit Lion. I kept the Lion in my left peripheral vision as I quickly looked at the perimeter bushes of the park on my right, which was about fifty yards away, and noticed my brother was way over there ducking and making his way through a tunnel in the bushes to get out of the park and onto the sidewalk next to the street. I had no idea how he got there so fast because he was just standing right next to me with his friend in what seemed to be like two seconds earlier.

I quickly focused back on the Lion with the thought it wasn't time for me to leave; I had no fear at all of what I was seeing because my Lord Jesus Christ had shown me visions of Spirits before. I remained still and calm as I listened to sounds of the groans that were coming from the direction of the Lion to me. I concentrated on the low sound that created a vibration that I could hear and feel throughout my whole body. It was like a powerful groaning coming from its chest. The sound gave me the feeling of peace and it put me at peace. The Lion was peaceful, and I felt like I loved this Lion. Then I felt a slightly stronger vibration coming from a deeper sound, and I thought that it was the Lion beginning to speak. At that moment, the Lion turned His face fully to the left and looked directly into my eyes. That's exactly what I wanted Him to do as I remained calm and maintained eye contact with Him.

My thoughts in my mind was that He was inviting me to look upon Him as much as I needed and wanted to, so that I would not have any doubt in my mind to remember every detail about our encounter, that everything I would see was real and has a purpose for understanding the truth about the Spirit of Light. That is when I realized that this was another vision for me to learn from. And this beautiful Lion appeared in Spirit before me to teach me what I wanted to know then, and what I needed to know from then on. So, I paid close attention to every detail so that I could never forget it.

The Lion's nature reminded me of when I would hear the voice of Jesus that sounded direct to a point, yet gentle and kind, just like the nature of the Angels that had appeared to me in the Robes of Light. Only this time, the Spirit Lion would be the first one to show me His face and talk to me the way my Lord Jesus Christ did with telepathy from that place of our whole minds. Then I believed that the Lion was my Lord Jesus Christ appearing in the form of a Lion to answer my questions, amazingly in the form of my most favorite animal. Although I wasn't sure yet why Jesus would appear in the form of a Lion although I was pleasantly surprised, at that time I felt that it didn't matter that He appeared in the form of a Spirit Lion, because I felt the Spirit of Jesus was inside the Lion that was conversing with me.

As I was looking at His eyes I began to speak the way I spoke to Jesus and Jesus spoke to me, by holding the whole thought in my mind that said everything I wanted to say at once, and I said, "show me your eyes; I want to see them up close". I knew He could hear and understand the thoughts that I was holding for Him. Immediately, His eyes appeared closer to me like I had telescoping vision, so that the eyes on His Lion face appeared to be about the size of my face. I couldn't see my hands or my body, I was just there at the stage in my mind and Spirit. Everything that happened and everything I saw, I looked at it as if I were to remember it forever.

Then I focused intently on His left eye and saw it perfectly clear, like I could see everything in focus all at the same time while I listened to the groans from His chest. He was showing me His Lion eye in vivid colors that I had never seen or could see that way in the world. First my eyes traced the black ring encompassing around His eye on His eyelids. Then, I saw the glowing bright pure golden color of His iris. I looked intently at His iris and noticed between the pure gold lines there seemed to be a brighter light gleaming out from behind it. The Light appeared to be reaching out between the lines of gold, as if calling me to show me that it was the Living Spirit of Light. Then I asked in my mind to see the other side of His iris to be in His eye with the Spirit Light and I immediately passed through it and entered in to see that there was a pure living Spirit of Light that filled His entire eye. The thought that came to my mind is simply described by the word, beautiful, and the feeling that came from the Light entirely engulfed me. It was the same as the light when I peered into the Robes of Light as it filled my room, only a little brighter when I was in it. Then, I thought, I want to see the other side of the eye and be in the body. So, I passed through the back of the eye and entered into the body of the Lion. And I saw that it was also all entirely pure Living Light without any darkness or shadow anywhere within it. I could see that the Living Light was in the exact form of the Lion, and I was in Him. I focused my vision to look outside of the Lion body, when I noticed that I could see the chairs stacked against the right inside wall of the stage as if I were viewing it by standing on the stage inside the Light of the Lion, but my body wasn't there with me, I was invisible and weightless. When I had seen all that I believed that I needed to see and experience, which was the peace and love in the Pure Light of the Living Spirit of Life, I carefully retraced my way back into the center of the eye and through the iris for one last time to peer at the pure golden iris as the Living Light of the Spirit of Life peered out to me one last time for me to remember it. Then I traced around His whole eye, following the black ring encircling His eyeball once again. After I finished looking at His beautiful Lion Face, I returned to my body to see HIM from the same distance I did before from where my body was still standing by the tree. There appeared to be a blurriness like a heat wave rising over both His eyes as we turned and looked away from each other at the same time.

I had looked over to the bushes where my brother exited the park. Then I momentarily looked back at the face of the Lion as He turned His face toward me at the same time to show me one last thing before I left. He showed me a Blood Red Fire covering each of His eyes concealing them both completely from sight. The Lion slightly moved His face up to acknowledge me and said, "I will be with you for the rest of your life." Then He brought His face back down to normal after He finished talking. I moved my face up and down as He did, to acknowledge what my Lord Jesus Christ last said before we both looked away from each other at the same time. I could see His brightness on the stage in my peripheral vision as I ran toward the tunnel in the bushes hoping that I could catch up to my brother and his friend since I knew they ran out of the park at least fifteen minutes earlier.

As I was crouching down making my way through the tunnel in the bushes, which was about eight feet wide, I felt so happy, excited, and giggly inside to the point of where I couldn't help laughing out loud to myself. It finally happened that after all those years, I finally had witnesses to see the Spirit Realm that I had talked about before. This would be my first opportunity to say to my brother, I told you the Spirit is real. And remembering how amazing the vision was to have seen Jesus in the form of a Lion of Light, and all the things that He let me see, at the same time I couldn't wait to tell my brother and his friend the rest of what happened.

When I crossed over to the other side of the street and onto the sidewalk, I saw something different for the first time. I saw my brother and his friend about twenty yards away from me running at an impossible super-fast motion speed until they were about one hundred yards away; meanwhile I felt like I was running in slow motion while I watched them. As I thought about it, I was seeing them run the distance that they had already run in the past, until they got to the actual distance that they were supposed to be from me when I first looked toward them, then we began running at the same speed. That was the funniest thing I ever saw, and it made me start laughing so hard that I had to stop and take a breather. It was comical for me to see them running together in fear from the sight of the Lion, that I could barely catch my breath from laughing out loud at the sight of them running away so fast. When they heard me, they looked back and waited for me in shock of what they saw. But I had no fear at all, only the memory of peace and love while I felt enlightened by the Spirit of my Lord Jesus Christ again.

When I caught up to them, my brother's friend still had a frightened look on his face when he asked me, "what was that?" And I said, "it was a lion ghost." I looked at them and told them in a calm voice, "Don't worry we are never going to do that again. We all agreed and walked home. I didn't mention to them everything that I saw except that I could see the chairs behind the Lion through its Spirit body. We confirmed that we all saw the ghost on the stage and left it at that. For some reason, I never saw my brother's friend again.

I had a challenging time with this vision because no one else I knew or ever would know has ever witnessed a vision like this one. Specifically, something they had interacted with had left them with a mystery to figure out over time. And I learned that this gave me a unique perspective of what my Lord Jesus means by the words, "Seek and you shall find." The truth is there is no end to that passage; we must always look to find the truth in everything we say and do because we need divine guidance to become divine with His help.

This is the language of the Heavenly Realm of the Spirit. I can explain the interpretation and the meaning of this vision for those that seek the truth to understand what I was taught so far. It is proving to be a masterpiece of a vision that was being held back in secret for another day and age. Apparently, the day and time for the revelations of visions has come to pass. And the order of unfolding the interpretation of a vision in a Chosen One's life is just as important as to bring an understanding of the answers to its full meaning. This is the best way to learn by the Word of Truth about what is happening in this Realm of Matter as we discover its boundaries of limitations compared to the unlimited Realm of the Spirit.

It is forever in my heart, as a Chosen One, to continuously contemplate the Word of truth, visions, symbols, sounds, dreams, vibrations, and signs that are given to me to learn, believe, and express to the best of my knowledge for myself and for others to have faith; that all creation belongs to GOD, including each one of us who are in it, whether we believe it or not. I can only tell others the things that have been shown to me by my Lord Jesus Christ, which have led to my enlightenment up to this point, and how I have been led by the Holy Spirit to the proper interpretations throughout the course of my lifetime since they have been revealed to me at their proper appointed times. Understand that the plan of our GOD the Father through HIS Son Jesus Christ, for perfecting all things to their proper place in time, cannot be rushed.

Also be aware that visions can be completely understood within the fraction of a second, as if time stands still for that knowledge of events to spiritually fill you instantly. Or their meanings may be given to you part by part at separate times as you experience the truths in them throughout time for you to spiritually mature by them in phases as your understanding of the knowledge grows according to your faith. That may be because they may have several overlapping related meanings, and trying to know them all at once could be confusing. They come to us with the Spirit of Enlightenment that fills us up, and our Spirit becomes just that much brighter as we accept each experience throughout time.

Visions evolve into revelations over time as knowledge is gained. Like when the evidence that is discovered about history can be used to prove it in diverse ways for more in-depth knowledge of the past. That brings more insight for the reasoning to believe in the Word of Truth: that only the beholder may be able to recognize the validity of the truth in it, because it was meant only for them to know the way that the Chosen One will understand it. Nothing can be guessed or forced; it is a gift of enlightenment that no one can boast about.

As a recreation of the Spirit in humanity and given the Chrism of the Child by my Lord Jesus Christ, I will continue to learn and become more Spiritually powerful throughout the course of the end times. Everyone that looks to find knowledge from listening, learning, believing, and following the Holy Spirit may find the hidden mysteries from this vision useful to tie into something they may have been shown or will be given to know, while learning to know the Truth in my Lord Jesus Christ, the Word of GOD.

Focus and contemplate on the Word of Life in Spirit prayer and believe in Him unconditionally, so that you will have eternal life by having Him living in you in Complete Unity. Remember the Testimony Of GOD: GOD has given us eternal life, and that life is in HIS Son Jesus Christ; whoever has the Son Jesus Christ has life, and whoever does not have the Son of GOD, who is Jesus Christ, does not have life.

One of the greatest of Spiritual strengths that I learned from my Lord Jesus Christ through the Holy Spirit seems to come from cultivating the ability to harness patience within me as I wait for His voice to speak to me. Patience is practiced for readily waiting for the next sign, symbol, vision, or word of instruction to come out from the Heavenly Realm, outside or from within us.

VINCENTE GARCIA

We must be ready and willing to move forward with that hidden knowledge to mature in Spiritual growth. Just like the love from our Lord Jesus Christ, once you have Him within you, you have Him with you in Complete Unity forever by keeping His commands. You are in Him and He is in you as One in Spirit forever. Having Him is truly the only way to always remain living in the Spirit to ultimately achieve perfection with Him and by Him.

Anyone who thinks otherwise has been fooled by someone else or by themself. Either way they are living a foolish life to their own demise to die twice. First in the flesh body, then in the spirit, which is the Second Death of doom and destruction for that person's spirit that refused to live by the New Covenant of the Spirit of my Lord Jesus Christ while in the Realm of Earth.

As a Chosen One, we must live on earth now as we must live in heaven later. That is what a Chrism Child of Light naturally wants to do. We are all children learning to walk and talk in Spirit to our GOD the Father through HIS Son Jesus Christ. The evidence for that truth we can see in babies and children that look at us with that pure truth and lack of corruption in their eyes. Like nothing in the world matters but you when they know you love them. That is how our Lord Jesus Christ sees us, because He knows that it is what we once were as a newborn child, and He knows that we can relearn to become that mindset of perfect love by the enlightenment of His helping us. No one can do it alone; we must accept Him and have His help from the eternal life and love in Him to teach us. It is a Spirit of Power that enables the Chosen One to become Spiritually Resurrected into an enlightened Chrism Child of GOD through our Lord Jesus Christ.

As a Chosen One that was given the Chrism of the Child, I am not exempt from learning the truth any less than anyone else, only I have been given a responsibility to reveal what I have been given to show by the anointing gifts of the Holy Spirit at this time. I have been given the interpretation of these messages to help the Children being called to my GOD the Father through my Lord Jesus Christ for them to mature in Spirit at a much faster rate of understanding the Truth in the Word. This is a revelation to all my brothers and sisters in my Lord Jesus Christ for the End Times of this World. Eventually, we will all learn to mature into His perfection, to see all others in the same manner, and to suffer through helping them become sanctified by the Word of Truth from GOD, and then be anointed by HIS Holy Spirit and the Spirit of HIS Son Jesus Christ for salvation. This is knowing our GOD the Father and our Lord Jesus Christ: by accepting the gift of HIS salvation for us to have eternal life as we live as One with them through HIS Son, our Lord Jesus Christ.

Chapter 6- Searching Spirit Knowledge

As I grew up into my high school years, I didn't get any definitive answers that I was searching for from anyone I knew about what it means to have seen and encountered a Spirit. Some people would talk about ghost encounters: that they heard about someone who died and visited someone else they knew. They could only guess why at best or tell what they imagined in a vague explanation that ended in something like they really don't know. Others would repeat common verses from the bible that they heard of, but live like they didn't believe them anyway. Some would rather ignore what I had experienced or change the subject when I began sharing details about spirits.

I realized there are two types of believers: those that decide to seek how to believe in the truth, and those that decide to seek how not to believe in the truth. Maybe the non-believers were in denial or they felt like they were in danger of believing it is true, which would force them to change the narrative of their life from what they desire it to be. I noticed that the fastest way to disperse a crowd is to start talking about my Lord Jesus Christ and all the wonderful ways He fulfills my life every day. There aren't many that can speak the truth from experience and bring the truth out from the heart because it isn't fully understood by them in that way.

After being shunned by people who couldn't help me with Spirit knowledge, I really lost the drive to share the details of my Spiritual encounters, mostly because I learned that people are literally ignorant to the core when it comes to visions and spirits, and especially to the truth in Spirit knowledge. And that's when I came to the realization that some people don't mind living in ignorance and in a lie, with no interest in understanding the truth to gain the wisdom of life. Not that they were all bad people, but because they just didn't see any value in learning what it is to become a Holy in Spirit person and they have no genuine inspiration to want to actually live that way.

Some people relate being a good Spiritual person to what brings evil or living cursed if they get into it. They fear the thought of having someone bring up the subject like it's taboo amongst friends. People literally run away from trying to live a good Spiritual life believing it's impossible to stay with it to become perfect. And that is believing a lie. So, they just stop trying to learn the truth.

I realized I was alone in this belief of having and seeking Spiritual perfection, and I had no one to talk to about it —at least, not anyone with a sense of purpose to be motivated to seek the truth in the Word of GOD to live in perfection now. That to me is a non-believer with low self-esteem, laziness, complacency, pride, cowardice, and anti-Christ. The bottom line is that anyone who refuses to learn and follow the commands of my Lord Jesus Christ and accept to live in the New Covenant of the Spirit is anti-Christ and condemned on Earth. That is why my Lord Jesus Christ taught me to know the whole world is condemned unless the Chosen One answers to His authority and accepts Him for eternal life.

The inspiration to overcome this problem came to me when I thought that if I could find a way to prove it for myself by the undeniable truth in the Words of Jesus Christ, and learn to explain it to others using their own bibles that they say they believe in, then the ignorant may have a chance to become inspired and turn to our Lord Jesus Christ and keep His commands the way I was learning to. From what I was taught in Spirit, I knew, believed, and understood until it became impossible for me not to believe in the Word of Truth. I know there must be some kind of mistake in the interpretations or the way the truth was being served up to the people learning that keeps them in confusion and ignorance. I will never let what I know go, because their lives and my own depend on knowing the Word of Truth.

Firstly, I needed to learn everything I could about the spirits in the bible. Secondly, I needed to somehow produce tangible evidence that there would be such a strong compelling argument, that it would prove that it must be true, leaving them with no other choice but to be convinced and inspired to change their minds and seek to live Spiritually. That is what I set out to do at that time.

I started asking what the best bible was to read. At that time, the majority answer was the King James Version. I just learned how to read and write in modern English, and the most important thing that I had set out to learn about in my life was translated in some language no one commonly speaks today. It was ridiculous trying to get the true meaning of a foreign language that no one spoke anymore. And it was comical to hear the response I got when I started speaking that way to people who claimed to be religious. No one I knew wanted to speak that way, and neither did I. But I went through it anyway, reading out loud to make sure I was pronouncing the words, sometimes finding myself wondering what was coming out of my mouth.

When I finished the book, I thought out of everyone I knew or would know that I was the only one who ever read the King James Bible from cover to cover. So that became one of my primary questions: "Have you ever read the King James version bible from cover to cover?" I don't believe I ever heard a solid "yes." I got a whole lot of diversions that referenced other bibles or religions, made up excuses, or strait up expressed disinterest. So, I read those other bibles too. And of course I didn't want to leave out the book of Mormon, The New World Translation, and the Quran. The common consistency was that Jesus lived, and GOD is the Creator. And I'll let it be known now, anyone who says they know how to spell the name of GOD the Father by referring to scripture, has misinterpreted the bible and is misleading others to do the same.

After a while, I could tell that most people didn't take what they called their religion of choice seriously, and that those who did seemed to be confused in one way or another by how they were taught to believe without fact checking what was said by the Word of GOD. And it made me feel sad for people when I realized my Lord Jesus has been righteous to say the whole world is condemned, and I was making a list of why that statement is the truth.

But the fact is that no one could teach me the truth from beginning to end to save another person, nor were they interested in taking the time to just say it. Once again, it seemed to be too much trouble for people to explain. I once asked a priest to tell me who Jesus was and he said, "He is GOD." To his surprise, I told him, "That's not true." And my immediate question was, "Then who did He pray to?" His confession to me was, "I get paid to teach that in religion by the military and that's what I'm going to do." I looked at him in disappointment with the thought in my mind, "then you have your reward." That was when I ended our conversation. Usually, my conversations with false prophets ended in an invitation to their church, and that didn't work for me when I had so many questions on my mind that I knew no one following the doctrine of men had the answers to.

I wished better for humanity, and I wished that I could help them understand the truth that I knew even up to that point. I just didn't have all the answers for a complete understanding yet. I needed more information to have the ability to make my message to them effective in every way possible. I didn't even factor in telling people what I had experienced in my life, because I knew that it wasn't enough to just tell them that to inspire them to change their belief to the Word of Truth. I tried that, and it failed, so why would it make them believe? Look at everything my Lord Jesus Christ said and did in the New Testament, and it still seems like the whole world is condemned for not believing those things, which proves Him right that way. It hurts me just to think about how people reject Him, and it brings me to tears because I love Him so much. And speaking my testimony proved to be repellant to most of my friends, except the ones who knew I wouldn't lie to them and to this day they are still One Family with me in my Lord Jesus Christ.

I occasionally would be asked, which book is the best of all those you read, and why? The truth is all the books were good to learn because they all speak of GOD and

Jesus Christ. That's one way I was maturing from all that reading, learning, believing, and understanding. But I came to the conclusion that we are not going to find salvation from knowing all the scriptures in all the bibles. We must understand the possibilities of how the Holy Spirit and our Lord Jesus Christ speaks to us to teach each of us individually throughout our lifetime while using what is written as a guide to manage ourselves living by the Spirit in the flesh and doing what is required of us in this day and age while my Lord Jesus is leading us to the Word of Truth through the Holy Spirit within us. There is no single way for everybody to learn the truth in the Word of Truth because we all are living extremely complicated lives, and our train of thought gets developed differently and uniquely. Therefore, the only way for anyone to learn the Truth in the Word is through my Lord Jesus Christ who will communicate to us individually through the Holy Spirit specifically the way each individual can understand it to live for eternal life. My message is to bring what is consistent and a complete understanding of the Gospel my Lord Jesus Christ taught me without denominational doctrines of mankind. I'm with my Lord Jesus Christ in Complete Unity first and foremost and anything else is a waste of my time unless it helps me to keep His commands and helps others turn to Him and do the same.

Then I began to realize that I was working from a completely different level of inspiration that I couldn't prove by words alone. So, my focus narrowed in on learning what is consistent in all the bibles concerning living by the Spirit of our Lord Jesus Christ -by stripping away all the burdens of lies that aren't commands from our Lord Jesus Christ to teach others how to be like Him- so there is no way to be turned away from Him and live with eternal life.

Now, I had to gather all the books that teach about my Lord Jesus Christ for comparisons and put the case together in a way that made perfect sense for people to understand the way of the Holy Spirit and the Spirit of our Lord Jesus Christ by knowing the purpose of His sacrifice for us in this Earthly Realm and what is expected of us by Him.

There was only one thing that I thought that I must do to solidly close my case which was to produce tangible evidence that proves that GOD loves us all and speaks to us through HIS Son Jesus Christ in unlimited ways of signs, symbols, visions, dreams, sounds, vibration, and telepathy. HE provides for us, HE answers our prayers and grants us our hidden wishes, and HIS will is to give us all eternal life. That is how my search began as I followed the guidance of the Holy Spirit. And with all of that, off I went in search of learning how to lead others to my Lord Jesus Christ for His true Spirit knowledge to have Spiritual enlightenment.

Chapter 7 - Tangible Evidence

As I was combing through the bibles looking for consistencies in the Word of Truth, I always had something in the back of my mind, which was the thought that it would be impossible for me to prove to someone else that GOD and Jesus Christ had shown me visions to give me unshakeable faith in them. But I knew that the Angels of my Lord Jesus Christ were constantly working to pave the way to help establish the steps of this Chosen One, to bless me, and let me know they are always watching over me.

For example, I began to notice a sign from the Spirit when I would be driving my car on the freeway or on a neighborhood street and a random streetlight would go out right when I crossed directly underneath it. And the first thing that came to my mind was that the Angels were letting me know they were watching over me. After a few times, it had become a common thing for me to look forward to what I called little miracles from GOD to help keep me filled with a strong Spirit and faith in HIM. It would happen at various times and places, and I never failed to think of the Holy Angels and Jesus when it did. That was what triggered my mind to always look for a sign to remember who was with me and what was happening in my life.

VINCENTE GARCIA

Knowing that I was living in Spirit, I never tried to manipulate that power for my own benefit because I knew it wasn't me doing it, nor did I ever feel like I had the power to do it myself for no reason. That would be disrespectful. It would usually take me by surprise, but sometimes my gift of Spiritual Foreknowledge would tell me to look ahead at the streetlights, because it was about to happen again. It was just a way for me to be reassured that everything is on track, and I was right where I was supposed to be practicing doing the right thing. I felt closer to Jesus when I got those random messages.

I remember I once had a friend with me in the car and I told him what would happen in advance to see if he would get to be a witness to it, and it did happen. That was just a little more reassurance for me to know that it's ok to share with some people. I would tell them, "That's GOD letting me know that we are in the right place at the right time."

In my mind, I would think to myself, "Lord, I know you have something you want me to do. I feel safe with you, and I'm just waiting for you to let me know what to do and when to act." This is how I learned to trust in my GOD the Father: by listening for HIM to speak to me. When it was time, HE would answer me to let me know HE had heard my prayers and then HE would prove to me that HE undoubtedly answered it all through my Lord Jesus Christ and the Holy Spirit with me.

TANGIBLE EVIDENCE

All the blessings that fell into my lap I acknowledged as blessings from my GOD the Father. It seemed to be passive for others as they would think it was just a coincidence. I felt like I needed more proof that GOD was with me, something tangible and with impossible odds to be undeniable in the minds of men. Of course, I knew that anything is possible with GOD.

I started to pray to GOD for a vision and a sign. I needed to know beyond the shadow of a doubt that GOD will give me whatever I needed to glorify HIM. I asked HIM to show me a vision or something that I can show to people I knew, so they would know that GOD has answered my prayer by showing me something tangible through a vision. I kept the question that I asked in my mind with all my heart because I had the faith and the patience to wait for it as long as I needed to. But I couldn't be disrespectful by not showing that I'm waiting and seeking the sign. I had to have that prayer in my mind and remember it by heart at all times as I just kept waiting.

I would finish my last class in high school and wait until everyone left campus before I would leave. It was my way of watching how time passed by while remembering that I was waiting for a sign. I became calm, quiet, and still like I was when I saw my Lord Jesus Christ appear to me in the form of a Spirit Lion of Light. I told all my family and friends that I was praying for a vision from GOD whenever they mentioned that they noticed the drastic change in my mood. They sometimes called it soul searching. I would just ignore that, because I knew exactly who I was and that I am recreated me in Spirit, inside and out.

At the end of one school day, I was walking through the campus as usual to check if everyone had left. I was about to leave when I noticed a school dictionary that was left on a concrete planter seating area under a tree. I knew no one was on campus, but I looked around anyway to see if I missed anyone. Just as I thought, no one was there but me. I picked up the book and fanned through the pages looking for a book marker or anything in writing so I could return it to the person who left it there, but I didn't find anything in it. It was a standard issue school dictionary that looked like new. I was meaning to pick one up anyway for homework and to help me with words for my bible studies. So, I held on to it for my studies.

Every so often I would just think of a word and look up the definition to see how its meaning was explained in detail by the experts of the world. Then a thought came to my mind to look up the word vision. Since I was waiting for a vision from GOD, I should at least know every definition of the word from the experts of this world. The question I had in mind was, "Would this book explain vision as I was taught by my Lord Jesus Christ what vision means?" So, I looked it up in a hurry to see what it said. I read it and was disappointed that it didn't say anything about Spiritual visions from GOD.

TANGIBLE EVIDENCE

But then I noticed something unusual that caught my eye. This dictionary had a list of words across the very bottom of the page for each page, and the lower right corner of the page was folded over covering the last word at the lower right corner. It was not just folded over; it was folded over and cut that way at the factory when they made it. The fold was in the shape of a triangle when the corner was cut with the excess paper folded over perfectly flat, so I carefully opened the fold with my fingernail to see the word that was covered, and the word was "Vision". I instantly had a feeling of relief in my heart, that it was my tangible sign from GOD and the answer to my prayer that I had been waiting for, for so long. I, without a doubt, knew in my heart that GOD had answered my prayer, and had given me a tangible sign that I could use as tangible evidence to prove to the people who knew I was waiting for tangible evidence from my GOD the Father to know HE answers my prayers. I asked for it, just like my Lord Jesus Christ taught me to ask, -to glorify HIM- and HE gave it to me.

I carefully checked the rest of the book, and there was not another page in the dictionary cut that way, folded, or damaged. Contemplating the possibilities of how this could happen for me specifically waiting in prayer for a tangible sign and vision, I knew that I was given that sign through my Lord Jesus Christ and that it was undeniable to me in a personal way because it helped me believe with a stronger faith that I was given the gifts of many visions that have continued coming into my life. It gave me the feeling that I was still in tune with my Lord Jesus Christ, and that all I needed to do was ask my GOD the Father, in the Name of HIS Son, my Lord Jesus Christ, to glorify my GOD the Father and it would be manifested. I was so happy, and I couldn't wait to tell everyone that I was relieved from my search and that my wait was over.

As a Chosen One living in Spirit with enlightenment from knowledge, I have the patience and forever unshakeable faith in HIS Son Jesus Christ. Ask for anything that can glorify GOD, and you shall receive it; that is the undeniable truth. I thank GOD in the Name of HIS Son Jesus Christ in every moment that I can to eternalize that they are always with me in every way, helping me throughout my life.

I have come to the conclusion that everything that I have received that was given to me in Spirit by the Holy Spirit, no matter how it is interpreted, is tangible evidence that is placed in me for eternal life, regardless of whether it's visible matter or not. There is no difference to me pertaining to which realm I have received visions from anymore. It's mine for the power of eternal enlightenment.

If and when you believe in GOD and have HIS Son in you, you will have all the same as I do, and more by your own personal experiences that will enhance your own gifts of Chrism by our Lord Jesus Christ through the Holy Spirit within you as One with your Spirit. Only, you will have received it in a way that is specifically designed just for you because you are uniquely created for the purpose that only you can fulfill as the person that you are being refined to become in your recreation. You are tangible evidence and no one will ever be able to shake you from believing in the power of the Life that is in our Lord Jesus Christ. We are all constantly learning as Children of Light that we are created from and of the Eternal One of Light through HIS Son, and that our possibilities are infinite and without end through having HIS Son our Lord Jesus Christ with us in Complete Unity. We are the living tangible evidence from the Living Light of GOD.

Chapter 8 - The Realms

After completing high school, I was at a crossroads to determine what adventure my Holy Spirit life would lead me through. I did not want to stay in one place all my life; I wanted to see the people of different cultures in the world for myself: how they lived, why it was important for them to keep their way of life, and what they believed in Spiritually compared to what my Lord Jesus Christ was teaching me. Most of all I wanted to be self-supportive and definitely independent with an open mind while comparing my understanding of the truth to other modern day religious practices, as I continued to seek for the answers to understanding the visions I experienced during my Spiritual enlightenment. Having the means to travel the world was definitely a must-have for me.

Before I embarked on this quest, I felt the need to spend more time with my immediate family and get well rooted in my beliefs in the value of family life to have something fresh in mind to bring to the table as I made new friends and acquaintances. I realized I had become somewhat brash in my message to others about the Realm of the Spirit as I was in a bold and firm belief in my Lord Jesus Christ by my experiences. I didn't want to project myself in that way to others even though it was because I found it unacceptable that most people didn't believe to live openly in a Spiritual relationship with the Holy Spirit the way I had been taught to in Spirit.

I wanted to learn the diversity of how people came into their own Spiritual existence to see if it was possible to share a comparison of their beliefs with mine by using the principles of the Word of Life from our Lord Jesus Christ that was also written in the bibles without coming across as condescending. I needed to learn His nature of how to speak to others in that way that He does to remove the veil from their faces to clearly understand the truth in the Word of GOD for salvation.

So, I decided to decompress from the hustle of academic learning institutions for a year and just meld into whatever I could learn from the bible to gain wisdom. I picked apart the characters of the most favored ones in the bible and learned that most throughout history lived a life around people that were a mess in relation to knowing GOD. That's when I learned that no matter how intelligent people were, they had just as much fallacy in their character if not more than their own intelligence living in this realm that hindered the slightest understanding of living in the Spirit. Just look at how many times their cities and temples were destroyed. I know that fallacy becomes manifest in any individual not strictly adhering to the principles in the commands of my GOD the Father through my Lord Jesus Christ as we are expected to do- myself included. I was just getting started in learning the way to act with others by the way HE would expect me to. As a Chosen One, I am not exempt from bearing my own cross to become refined in living in the Spirit to stay free of sin. I needed to learn how to adapt to HIS nature in this modern day and age that I was living in this realm on earth.

I couldn't figure it out by all the rules laid out in the bibles for others throughout time. Let's be perfectly transparent in the truth and say that the modern way of life is more complicated and confusing by the distractions we have now compared to the simple past way of life, let alone all the different doctrines of religions throughout all the churches in the world. They were literally in competition with each other for thousands of years, to the point that they all have lost the point of living by the Spirit of GOD by HIS will to always love each other.

So I began to think that there must be something missing in all the religious sects, or that they may have been convoluted by the Dark Realm of evil powers over time to keep people from knowing the truth in the Word of GOD. Therefore, they have kept people from being able to enter into the Spirit Realm to live in Complete Unity. I saw that as a huge fallacy of religion compared to what I read in the bible of how we must worship GOD. It remains in my mind that it has been just too complicated for people to keep up with all those traditional laws, and that no one could be saved by it anyway while living in this realm of corruption.

I felt so much sorrow to learn that people in the world would even go to war and kill each other over religious doctrines that were man made. My understanding of what I called worshiping is to do it with love, beauty, and kindness for humanity by the will of GOD the Father. Everything is under the power of GOD for the love of GOD, so why couldn't we all believe and live that way? I understand that we need to protect our children from the harm of evil people, and that it is a necessity to have protection by all means. But to fight with people over believing in a peaceful religion is sacrilegious to the Word of GOD, without a doubt, if they claim to believe in the Living GOD. I was really hurt by that as I kept trying to make sense of what I should do living in Spirit the rest of my life. I just wanted to please GOD and be in HIS love by helping others believe in the Word of Truth.

That is when it came to me in prayer that I had to make it my first and foremost priority to live my life in the nature of GOD the Father like my Lord Jesus Christ did. There is no other way to please GOD than to be like HIS Son whom HE loves. He lived on this Earthly Realm like He lives in the Heavenly Realms. So, I narrowed it all down and tossed out the Old Testament Laws of Moses, "Mosaic Law," to live by the New Testament of our time: specifically by the Testimony of GOD concerning HIS Son Jesus Christ, the Law of the Spirit. If you have Jesus Christ, you have eternal Life. I learned what not to do from that Old Testament history and now I moved on to learn to live in the New Testament by the New Covenant of the Spirit with my Lord Jesus Christ the Son, to do the will of my GOD the Father.

I didn't see anything complicated about that; I just needed to start adjusting my life to live by the Spirit in this Earthly Realm while in the flesh while keeping my mind focused on what it is to live in the Heavenly Realm in Spirit as much as possible at the same time. Of course, I would have to continue to practice living that way every day and that would take time and effort as I suffered myself to make myself keep HIS commands. So, I decided to read anything that was written about my Lord Jesus Christ for myself to learn to understand and practice living by what He said consistently throughout all the scriptures in every bible book I could find.

One day, as I was in Spirit prayer, I asked my Lord Jesus Christ to give me something to do for Him. I wanted to know if I was ready to help someone and if He wanted me to do something for Him. So, I held that prayer as I kept myself listening, and He told me to leave the house and go in the direction I was guided. I got dressed and walked out of the neighborhood that I was living in while I was constantly searching for what I had to do. I came to the main highway and crossed it where there

VINCENTE GARCIA

was a line of retail businesses. I scanned across the parking lots and saw a sweet little old lady standing between the cars, holding her purse in her arms. My Lord Jesus Christ told me to gently approach her. So, I waved at her and said hello from a distance, and with a worried look on her face, she said hello to me. Then I asked her, "Are you ok?" And with her sweet little voice she said, "No, I locked my keys in my car, and I don't know what to do. I can't get home." Then I said, "Okay, let me see if I can help you get your keys out." I looked through the window of the driver side door, and noticed it had a large push button lock. I thought that if I could only find a way to get that lock pulled up, it would open. Immediately, I started to search for something on the ground in the parking lot, and found a wire coat hanger laying in the street a few cars away. I straightened it out, made a small hook on the end of it, pushed it into the car past the rubber seal around the window, caught it on the lock button, and then pulled it up to unlock her car door, so she was able to drive home right away. That is when I learned that we must seek to use the knowledge and power of the Heavenly Realm to help those in need in this Earthly Realm of matter because we have been given access to both realms while living in Spirit with the Holy Spirit who guides us.

Those that live in the ignorance of sin, fear, and doubt allow the demonic spirits of the Dark Realms to slip into them, and until they go to our Lord Jesus Christ to repent for forgiveness to receive the Chrism of the Holy

THE REALMS

Spirit, they have no protection coming from the Heavenly Realm of GOD. In some cases, the people in need of help will be left stranded, and may not make it home because someone did not repent of their sins to walk in the Spirit. The responsibility of each Child of GOD is to help others in need and to get them home safe to our GOD the Father through HIS Son Jesus Christ as we are being guided by HIS Holy Spirit.

In this Earthly Realm of matter, we need to learn to live in the Spirit within us to keep up with the Holy Spirit of the Heavenly Realm of Light and repel the dark spirits of the Dark Realms away from ourselves and our brothers and sisters. Only by having our Lord Jesus Christ within us in Spirit now is it possible to be recreated a second time to become truly alive to live Holy in the Spirit while we are in this Earthly Realm. Therefore, through our Lord Jesus Christ, we become alive in Spirit to die alive in Spirit as our Body-Temple passes away in this Earthly realm.

Because we received the Resurrection by the Chrism of our Lord Jesus Christ, and by that Chrism we are recreated alive in Spirit, which is called being born again, recreated, or reborn. By becoming reborn, we are then able to be Redeemed to live eternally in the Kingdom of GOD, as our GOD the Father has promised to us for keeping HIS commands. HIS Holy Spirit will raise us up alive to be transformed, at that time, into a new Spirit-Body like our Lord Jesus Christ is Spirit-

VINCENTE GARCIA

Body. And by the Holy Spirit, we will be taken into the Spirit Realm. Until we are transformed, we are learning to live our Holy Spiritual eternal life in this Earthly Realm now, as we will continue on to live our Holy Spiritual eternal life in the Spirit Realm of Heaven.

Chapter 9 - Commitment

I once had a false belief in my mind that as long as I was a loyal and hard worker, no matter what field I chose to work in, I would be able to build myself a great life and live happily ever after. All I had to do was be a good person. The saying, "there are two sides to every coin," is a great metaphor to remember when trying to get a life. I got to experience a lot of life in travel, sports, recreation, love, and war, but no matter how committed I was to making it better and building it up to its highest success, I got to see it all tumble down like it never existed.

I love life, but I also have learned that this world has nothing to offer that is everlasting. Because there is one guarantee in this Earthly Realm; that is you will get to see it get worse as your health does. So, we shouldn't get attached to the things of matter that we collect here because there won't be a moving truck behind your Hearst on the way to your grave for you to take them into the Spirit Realm. The only thing we are left with when we die is our final commitment to the New Covenant of the Spirit that we decided to keep in truth. And for me, it is to be committed to having eternal life in Complete Unity with my Lord Jesus Christ because the meaning of life is to have life. And my Lord Jesus Christ is the Light of Life. And no one can have eternal life without first becoming committed to having my

VINCENTE GARCIA

Lord Jesus Christ. I believe in the New Covenant of the Spirit, which is the Testimony of our God the Father, who is the Father of all creation including HIS Son our Lord Jesus Christ: the way, truth, and life. HIS choice for us is for us to accept by our own decision to receive HIS Son, as our Lord Jesus Christ, and receive HIS Holy Spirit, which come out from within HIMSELF to live within our Spirit as One for eternal Life now, as we live in this Realm of Earth within our Body-Temple of flesh.

At about the age of twenty-seven, I was finished living a military life, and I was about to try my skills in the civilian sector. Just before I exited, I prayed to my GOD the Father in the Name of my Lord Jesus and committed my life to HIM. I was done trying to live the way I wanted to and asked HIM to put me in the places that He wanted me to live and work. I didn't care what it was. Because my country was reducing its military production of aircraft, I left that field of work and I started with drywall construction and later found myself working retail management. After making a decent living at sales and leasing, I just got bored of sales even though it brought in twice as much income as I ever thought I would make at that time. I was committed to my work, and it really kept me busy, but I still didn't have a sense of fulfillment.

Once again, I prayed to GOD the Father, through my Lord Jesus Christ, and asked if He would put me to do the work HE wanted me to do so that I could have a sense of accomplishment and feel like I'm serving others for HIM. I never thought of what that could be; I just wanted to live my life committed to my GOD the Father and my Lord Jesus Christ.

One day, it came to me in a dream, around the age of forty-five, that I would be going to work in a place where there were a lot of lights, like in a warehouse with bright lights. That is when I knew I needed to keep myself ready to recognize the opportunity and move to the place where GOD wanted me to go to serve HIM.

Shortly after, I met the father of one of my coworkers who had retired from the Department Of Corrections as an Officer. He started his career at the age I was at that time, then worked for fifteen years and retired with a pension. All he did was travel around the country with his wife enjoying their life together. Right away I said, "I want to be that guy". If I had that job, I could retire in fifteen years and serve the Lord for the rest of my life without being too busy and tired every day from the hustle of business.

Not too long after that, I saw another coworker who was filling out an application for the Department of Corrections. I tried to talk him out of it because I knew he did well at the company we work for. When he said, "You can make twice as much money than you are making now and retire with a pension," I remembered my dream and filled out an application to begin testing for the department.

One year later, I was in the academy, ready to do what my Lord Jesus Christ wanted me to do. And of course I wasn't alone, I was following the path I was being led on by the Holy Spirit. And He made it known when I was in the initial orientation briefing that was held inside a prison housing unit. Before I was assigned a room, the Holy Spirit told me to look behind me over my left shoulder at room two hundred and twenty-two because that is where I was going to be assigned quarters. Of course, that is exactly the room I was assigned to, and that's how I knew by foreknowledge that I was exactly where I was supposed to be.

Working in a prison was not my idea of fun work although it was definitely built like a warehouse with a lot of bright lights like the Holy Spirit showed me in a dream-vision. I learned about all the vile things that men do to people and themselves. And I knew the Lord didn't put me there to be happy; He wanted me to live amongst the hidden evil and filth that people do that is prevalent in this world. I was put there to experience what could be the results of people not living by the Spirit. It didn't take long to learn that only the best of them valued living by the words that came out of their mouth. And they wanted to prove to be honorable, and in one way or another, they understood that living by their word was the last thing of honor they had left that

COMMITMENT

they could prove to be honorable to themselves. In prison, you do what you say you are going to do, or you are considered less than nothing by the people who know that you are a liar.

Even at the level of a highly confined society, people realize that a person is no good to anyone if they can't be trusted to act by the words that come out of their mouth, so they learn to choose their words carefully. I spent every day and night shift making sure they remembered that, and I would do the same for myself because I knew that I was being held accountable to the same standard.

As a Chosen One, my commitment is to live and die by my word while keeping the commands of my Lord Jesus Christ, which is the deed that I am expected to do to prove my love for GOD. I decided to give myself to my GOD the Father through my Lord Jesus Christ to guide me by the Holy Spirit to work wherever HE wanted to put me to serve HIM, that was my commitment that I asked for. Our tongue is like a two-edged sword, and by the words that come out of our mouths, we will live or die by it.

I use my words to prove and reprove the Truth in the Word of God for others to know Him because HIS will has become my will to bring all people that HE is calling to live for eternal life with HIM. I am committed to living by the Word of GOD until the day I die in my Lord Jesus

Christ. And by the Word of GOD in this Earthly Realm of matter, to live worthily now for later is to deserve to be raised up to HIM in the Heavenly Spirit Realm for eternal life. It is HIS promise to raise up all humanity who have accepted HIS Seal, which is HIS Holy Spirit deposited in us for the day of redemption, and also have the Spirit of HIS Son Jesus Christ in Complete Unity.

There is no other way except by committing our life to our GOD the Father through our Lord Jesus Christ and the Holy Spirit to live as One in Spirit with them. We must be refined in Spirit every day as we live committed by the Word of Truth to remain worthy of our Lord Jesus Christ in the way that He has taught us to keep His commands. This is living in a commitment by the New Covenant of the Spirit, who is our Lord Jesus Christ, and He is the Word of Truth given to us as a gift of eternal life by our GOD the Father.

Chapter 10 - The Enlightening

There are times in my life when GOD gave me more than what I prayed for because HE searches the heart of HIS Chosen One to comfort me in my time of need. HE knows what I need before I speak. And my prayers in Spirit to honor HIM are without a doubt heard without fail.

There was a woman who lived alone who had committed her life to our Lord Jesus Christ, and she asked HIM to bring her someone, as he saw fit, who would love her and care for her all the days of her life. She had been baptized in water to be forgiven for her sins, and asked our GOD the Father to receive HIS Holy Spirit through our Lord Jesus Christ. Then she vowed not to look for a husband or date people anymore if that was the will of our GOD the Father. About that time, I was in a place in my life where I just wanted to be loved by someone for who I am.

About three months later, after her prayer, we met at an annual memorial to honor those who passed away in the line of duty working as civil servants of the local area. She would later learn that this would be her first-hand testimony, and that when she made the commitment to turn her life over to our GOD the Father through our Lord Jesus Christ, the little miracles began to manifest so wonderfully in her life that her desire to praise our GOD the Father filled her heart daily. We are inspired to live our lives as a couple in Spirit with our Lord Jesus Christ together in Complete Unity.

After a couple of years, we were guided to move to another prison facility. It was in that area that we built our first house together. I was finally able to unpack my belongings for the first time since we moved in together. When I found my old study bibles, it sparked up a conversation about teaching her the word with daily bible studies. She was receptive to the idea and proceeded to tell me how she was shunned from attending the local church from where we met, due to her wearing dress pants to church that she had been told was forbidden. So, she stopped attending the church and stopped learning the Word. Although she still had the desire to learn the Word of GOD, she had trouble understanding the meaning of the truth in the scriptures.

In our conversation, she expressed how hard it was to understand the bible on her own, and that she needed help understanding the proper way of living in the Spirit. I assured her that our Lord Jesus Christ would help her learn to understand the Word if she asked in prayer for the guidance of the Holy Spirit to lead her to the truth. All she needed to do was ask a question in Spirit prayer the way she had first done, and then search for the answer so the Holy Spirit would lead her to the truth to enlighten her. She asked me a question about a

THE ENLIGHTENING

conversation we just had and wanted to know what the bible said about that subject. I picked up one of my Bibles and cracked it open for the first time in front of her, put my finger on the page that it was opened to and started reading. The verses I read answered her question exactly as she wanted to hear, and as I explained the verses, she understood them perfectly. She was surprised at what had just happened and asked me, "How did you do that?" I replied, "It's not me -it's the Holy Spirit that helped me open the bible to the page that has the Word of GOD written in it for us to learn from, and it's the Holy Spirit of God the Father that makes these things happen, and it happens all the time. As Chosen Ones, we are miraculously led to the truth by the Holy Spirit." She was amazed at the little miracle that had enlightened her mind and Spirit that much more.

I let her know that the bible I read from is an Old English translated bible, and that it would be better if she studied a bible that was written in her own modern English, so it would be much easier to learn and understand the meaning of the words. It so happened that a Christian coworker bought her a bible as a gift, and she began to read it every day. It is amazing to see a Chosen One grow into living in Spirit Light as they see the Holy Spirit working with them and showing them the things that mean the most to them in signs, dreams, symbols, sounds, visions, and vibrations to receive blessings for understanding Spiritual Knowledge.

VINCENTE GARCIA

Then there comes the enlightening of their mind and heart by the Holy Spirit, leading them to the truths that give them another sense of awareness that manifests their Spirit with the abilities to become the perfect person in Spirit, Mind, Heart, and Body-Temple. With our Lord Jesus Christ, we struggle, suffer, and persevere to overcome and master each task that we are given until we know the Truth in the Word to have it as truth forever written in our hearts. The heart is where the Mind of the Spirit speaks to us from, as our minds decipher the Word being spoken with the memory of what has been learned from following our Lord Jesus Christ speaking to us through the Holy Spirit. As Chosen Ones, we seek the little miracles that we look forward to every day as we mature, living in Spiritual Complete Unity.

As I like to say, my Lord Jesus Christ was all over me, and it was time for me to become a little more enlightened in Spirit after I had a new High Definition security camera installed on our house to record the actual timing of events if there was any movement. It was nice to have a security system since there was a lot of soliciting in the new housing tract back then. What really got my attention was how, between the time of four and five o'clock in the morning, the system would start recording a lot of activity, but didn't show anybody coming up to the front door and patio area.

THE ENLIGHTENING

I thought it was odd that it happened every morning, and I was curious if it was moths or birds flying close to the cameras, causing it to record movement. I viewed the videos and noticed there were a lot of lights flying around the camera like large flies, and then a thick light that I estimated to be the size of a softball, periodically flying through the camera view and disappearing into the ground. It would later come back out from the same place, which seemed unusual to me. I was able to slow the recording down to a second-by-second still frame setting to see if I could identify the insects so I could get the proper bug repellent. To my surprise, I was able to identify them as spirit orbs.

I contacted my lifelong friend, a Paleontologist and Shaman for the Chumash Native American Indians, and he mentioned that there is an ancient burial ground in that area, and that the spirit of the dead would travel toward the west. He had once been called to help in a government study of Spirit Orbs because they were trying to figure out what they were.

The real problem I was having is I could feel there were negative vibes being generated by them around my house, and I wanted them to go away. His suggestion was to encircle the property with burning sage in Spirit prayer with the thought of asking the Creator, which is how they refer to GOD in the Native American Language, to remove them from my property and check to see what happened the next morning. It did lessen the number of orbs being detected, but it didn't get rid of them all. My first thought was that maybe the remaining spirits were not all Native American spirits, but something far worse.

Then I began to contemplate the Word of Truth to ask for guidance about what I had done. I realized that I had conducted prayer in the old Native American traditional way, and not exactly as I should have, living in the New Covenant of the Spirit for this time period. So, I asked my Lord Jesus Christ for the understanding of these spirits. He told me to pray in the Spirit and ask our GOD the Father in Spirit prayer and in the Name of my Lord Jesus Christ, while encircling the property and entering every room, until the burning sage I was holding was completely burned away.

After I did exactly what my Lord Jesus Christ said to do and say, I never saw another detection of spirit orbs in the HD camera recording ever again. I was astonished at the power in the Name of my Lord Jesus Christ and enlightened that much more to a new level of enlightenment from understanding that knowledge. I had learned how important it is to praise my GOD the Father in the Name of my Lord Jesus Christ for HIS protection from evil in everything I do to glorify my GOD the Father.

I knew that the sage was not a requirement for my prayer to be answered, it just felt that much more beautiful to conduct the prayer in Spirit while offering the sweetest sage that had been prayed over for the blessings from my GOD the Father, while honoring HIM and my Lord Jesus Christ in the Name of my Lord Jesus Christ. That became my newest testimony of enlightenment, and I became that much brighter in Mind, Heart, Body-Temple, and Spirit as a Chosen One. The Holy Spirit became more active in my life in those days, and this was the showing of the Spirit strength within me from my Lord Jesus Christ.

One night, my wife and I carpooled to work for a night shift. As we passed through the first guarded perimeter gate of the prison, we entered into the prison grounds restricted area. We were about to walk down a long-gated sidewalk that was approximately two hundred yards long between two guarded security points. The walkway was lit up by several streetlights lined up all the way down one side of it. Before we started to walk through, I was told in Spirit to remind her about my testimony of the streetlights, from when I was in high school over thirty years earlier, and let her know that those kinds of signs were starting to happen again. Our Lord Jesus Christ told me to show her one of the streetlights halfway down the walkway, so I said to her, "Do you see that streetlight that the crowd of people in front of us are going to be walking under right now?" She answered, "Yes." Then I said, "Keep watching it as everyone crosses under it and it stays on, but when we walk under it, it will shut off, because we are exactly where our GOD the Father wants us to be."

We walked at a good distance behind everyone else as they crossed under the streetlight I had mentioned and when they made it to the other side, nothing happened. Then, a few moments later, as soon as we crossed under that same streetlight, it shut off. She was once again amazed to have witnessed what I had been telling her about what happened to me when I was a teenager. We were both enlightened together in Spirit that much more. We praised GOD in the Name of HIS Son Jesus Christ for all His little miracles that keep us as bright in Spirit as we can be in faith.

As a Chosen One, my mind must remain open in prayer every day, giving thanks to my GOD the Father in the Name of HIS Son, my Lord Jesus Christ. I was still searching for the meaning of our move to the new work facility that I was guided to. It was my foremost business to wait patiently for the messages of understanding that would be revealed to me at the right time, on GOD's time. I could feel a difference in the energy within me and all around me that was drawing me closer to my GOD the Father. It was reminding me of the nature living in the Spirit that I was familiar with in my young age, as I was learning from HIS Son Jesus Christ through the Holy Spirit.

I felt like I was getting tuned up, to stay keeping up with the guidance of the Holy Spirit, as He was becoming more active inside and outside of me more frequently. I was becoming more enlightened by my understanding that I have matured in Spirit since the time I had received my Chrism of the Child from my Lord Jesus Christ. My enlightenment is my testimony of the truth that I must put forth for others to become stronger in their faith, and enlightened by the Holy Spirit with the inspiration for eternal life that they must receive in their Body-Temple now. My command from my GOD the Father was becoming distinctly manifested before my eyes, and I humbly welcomed the mission in Spirit prayer with all my existence in faith without any fear or doubt. I was already experiencing the Spirit of Foreknowledge, and that is how I am enlightened in Spirit to do HIS will in the Name of my Lord Jesus Christ.

Chapter 11 - Knowing What

The Ministries within the general prison population appeared to be getting stronger as people were learning to deal with their personal problems by contemplating the Word of GOD. Some of the Chosen Ones within the general population that were ministering the Word of Truth on their own time were highly respected for their efforts in helping others with their Spiritual needs. I acknowledged them and encouraged the groups to keep learning together. Their uplifted Spirit proved to me that the Word of Truth in the Gospel of our Lord Jesus Christ was making a strong impact on the morale of the Chosen Ones living within the gates.

I was getting closer to the end of the timeframe in which I had planned to work and retire. Although a lot had changed since I made that wishful statement -the "I want to be that guy" statement- about fifteen years earlier. It was becoming a reality, and not by my choice, but by the choice of my GOD the Father who put me where HE wanted me to be, as I had also asked for in Spiritual prayer. It was only by my decision to follow HIS Holy Spirit within me to accept the choice of HIS will for me. I can do nothing in word or deed on my own as a Chosen One, and I do not desire to make choices for myself while living in service to my GOD the Father. As my Lord Jesus Christ has taught me to only serve my

GOD the Father, so I must always wait for HIS choice to be presented to me first by my GOD the Father through my Lord Jesus Christ as He speaks to me through the Holy Spirit to my Spirit in Complete Unity within me. Then I can honor them by accepting HIS gifts of Spiritual guidance and little miracles of blessings for me.

There was a movement by a group of Chosen Ones beginning to develop, and the Holy Spirit had compelled me to help them. We all prayed over the subject and decided to follow the guidance of the Holy Spirit in hopes of bringing us together at the appropriate time. I didn't know them, but that didn't seem to be my greatest hurdle. The question I had was how I was going to help them in their ministry when they were going to be dispersed to different parts of the country. That is when I thought to pray to my GOD the Father through my Lord Jesus Christ to just show me the way and what to do, and I would do it.

I was told to get ready for the impact of everything and keep my mind focused on ministering for GOD to every person that would listen and learn. My time was running out, and I always felt like I was way behind in making up lost ground. The people walking out of the prison church would strike up a conversation about faith, which would give me an opportunity to ask what they learned that day. They would usually give a basic answer to move on with their business.

Where was the cheerfulness of the Holy Spirit? It became obvious they were not being filled with the Spirit. It was just like they were going through the motions of just showing up at the church building and leaving with nothing. That is when it hit me that something needed to be done about that, and I had to find out what I could do from the position I was in. I did not want to see the faces of those who are poor in Spirit projecting their suffering from being poor, hungry, and thirsty from the lack of understanding the Word of Truth.

The message was becoming clear in my heart, mind, and soul that I was being lifted to a higher level of understanding and enlightenment -not just for myself, but for the enlightenment of others. I vowed that if I could help it, I would not let anyone down from understanding what I know is true. Everything that I have, I give to those who need the inspiration for eternal life. This is who I am, recreated me: as a Chosen One to do the will of my GOD the Father in the Name of HIS Son, my Lord Jesus Christ, and guided by HIS Holy Spirit.

For a few weeks, I was praying for the answer to help those in need of the truth. It came to me in a dream. I was told to first start teaching the Word in the Gospel of my Lord Jesus Christ to everyone who will accept it, and specifically about the five chapters in John, thirteen through seventeen. So, I started sending the chapters in parts, followed up by some facts and a prayer each day by text to everyone in my phone contacts. My good friends appreciated it very much. The list was growing, and the people started to tell us their testimonies about them and their families turning to my Lord Jesus Christ again and others for the first time, which was a good feeling, making it all worthwhile. My wife started finding people to send the Word of Truth to in her phone contacts, and it became a Ministry in our little group. The Holy Spirit was all over our friends, and we were praising our GOD through HIS Son, Jesus Christ, many times a day.

But it was exhausting to do everything by phone on the move while working double shifts. I had to come up with a better idea to keep the momentum if I was going to help more people in need. The fact was, I needed a vacation to clear my mind and regroup my thoughts in case I was placed in a position to move again. Vacation would free up some time to keep the Word going to my friends. And of course, our vacation led to ministering to people on the cruise ship and whoever we met who was willing to listen and learn. More and more often, random people that I met would mention that I needed to author a book, and they would buy it. That is when I got the feeling that this was becoming too much for texting by phone. I began to realize that I had to write this message in a book to get the Word of Truth out because that is what I was told to do, and I could not stop writing in prayer until the Holy Spirit gave me the sign to rest. This was a revelation for me to know and to understand that I was the Chosen One who had been enlightened to author a book that explains the Gospel of my Lord Jesus Christ in the way I was taught to live in Complete Unity by the New Covenant of the Spirit before I read the Bible. I knew exactly what I was commanded to do as I became closer with the Holy Spirit as my guide on my Spiritual path.

Chapter 12 - The Inspiration

I became aware of these signs that were pounding at my heart and mind to form me into something I needed to become. I had to meditate on all the things that had happened to me in my life; to conjure up every bit of faith, power, patience, and self-control within me, and then some, to have what it took to keep up with what I was expecting to happen soon. I was on track to receive a Spiritual Revelation, and there was no time for complacency. The time of the reckoning had come to prove my worthiness for a message from my GOD the Father through my Lord Jesus Christ for HIS Chosen Ones in the world to become enlightened by the Truth in the Word.

The feeling that I keep within me is that I am on my way to my GOD the Father through my Lord Jesus Christ, and it is also my will to take everyone I can help with me as I do HIS will. Everyone who is being called to repentance and salvation must be saved, bar none, because my life and the life of those who decide to hear, see, and believe in the Word of Truth depend on it.

I began to tell everyone that Jesus is with me now. When I entered a building, I would shout out, "Jesus is in the house!" When I released a group to pass through my gated area for breakfast or lunch, I said, "Come to

VINCENTE GARCIA

Jesus!" over the public address system because they had to pass through my guarded gate. No one gets through the gate unless they have authorization, just like my Lord Jesus Christ teaches. He is the gate and no one goes to the Father except through Him. I could see that there was a sense of enthusiasm when those words were heard. They would say to me with a big smile, "I'm coming to Jesus." That seemed to spark just a little more inspiration than usual, and I wondered, "How can I do more?" I was still waiting to find out when the time of action would come to trigger my ministry to my GOD the Father, with my Lord Jesus Christ and the Holy Spirit in Complete Unity with my Spirit. My patience is constantly at work in serving my GOD the Father.

I had faith that there were many lost souls that were turning to my Lord Jesus Christ by hearing that there were pockets of spiritual growth all over the prison where we worked, which were beginning to spread to their families on the outside.

There were some who hesitated to speak openly about the inspiration for eternal life that is delivered now by having our Lord Jesus Christ. I wanted to see the power of the Holy Spirit working through each person who was learning, and see Him jumping off of every believer that was inspired in their hearts, minds, and souls for everyone else to witness the work of our Lord Jesus Christ.

THE INSPIRATION

Once again, I turned to glorify my GOD the Father in the Name of my Lord Jesus Christ in Spiritual prayer to help me answer this question that I asked Him: "Show me the Holy Scriptures that I may share with people to help them become spiritually inspired now?" I believed that there is such a teaching that will do just that, and my Lord Jesus Christ revealed it to me to glorify our GOD the Father. I suffered to know it every day as I had waited in patience for the answers, as I held that prayer in my mind. It's one thing to know it is possible, and it's another to find a way to make it effective and inspiring for all people, and that is what was needed. The question was for me to be given the ability to live up to the answer of the prayer, if it was the will of my GOD the Father to show me how to live up to knowing the answer and doing HIS will by whatever it takes to make it effective to manifest the answer in a written book that explains HIS will for HIS Children to receive the Chrism of the Child through our Lord Jesus Christ.

I would remember when it came to me in a dream, and I was told to tell people to read and study John, chapters thirteen through seventeen. But this time, I was told that I had to find those who were Chosen Ones and then be ready to teach them anything they had questions about those chapters. I listened and obeyed my Lord Jesus Christ and did just that everywhere I went. If I saw someone reading the bible, I would ask them if they had read the book of John and if they knew the Testimony of GOD. I asked them to study John chapters thirteen through seventeen, which I believe is my most inspirational part of the bible to share with those who want to know the Word of Truth. I wrote it on the bulletin boards so all those who passed by would get my message and come to me for answers if they needed help, and they did.

After a week or two, I would start getting responses from several people. Some of the people in the study groups were telling me they had organized a special study group amongst themselves to study the five chapters, and that they had never seen the entire group praise GOD in the Name of HIS Son Jesus more than they saw that day. I asked one of them, "Did you feel the Holy Spirit at that time?" And he replied, "Yes, everyone did. It was amazing. I have never seen anything like it; everyone was up praising the Lord." That was the face of inspiration that I was looking for as I expressed my happiness for them and encouraged them to keep teaching it to everyone who wants to learn and be saved.

There was one person who touched my heart, he was a tall, slender, and elderly man who kept quiet to himself and spoke in a soft voice. It was late at night before lights out for the night as he stood outside with his cane, looking up at the night sky, staring at the stars. Just as I passed by him about ten feet away, he called my name to stop me, but he would not turn his eyes to me. We were alone as he kept staring at the stars when

THE INSPIRATION

he said, "You know, Garcia, I read those chapters you told me to read." I could hear his voice choke up just a little, and I said, "You did." I was curious as to what he would say next. He said, "Every time I read them, I feel so happy inside." And I could hear him take a breath like he was crying. Then I asked him, "You felt the Holy Spirit in you, didn't you?" He couldn't speak for a moment. He just kept looking up at the stars, slowly shook his head, then said, "Yes." I replied, "Good, I'm happy you have the Holy Spirit. Keep reading it." And he replied, "I will."

My heart goes out to everyone who becomes inspired by knowing the love of our GOD the Father and HIS Son Jesus Christ through the Holy Spirit. The Chrism is the Superior Baptism, which is being anointed with the Holy Spirit, in the Name of our Lord Jesus Christ, which comes out from our God the Father. And our Lord Jesus Christ can anoint anyone, anytime, anywhere, and in any conditions. Since our Lord Jesus Christ has been raised from the dead by the Holy Spirit of our GOD the Father, and is ruling as our King at the right-hand side of our GOD the Father, there is no longer any excuse for anyone not to live a Holy Life in Spirit now.

Those who keep the commands of my Lord Jesus Christ deserve Him, and those who do not keep His commands do not deserve Him. That does not mean we are not worthy as sinners to accept Him to deserve Him. The truth is: it means that unless you repent of your sins to accept His Spirit in you, and follow His commands, you do not deserve to have salvation by having His eternal life within Him living in you now, which is the Resurrection that every believer must receive before they die in order to be Redeemed; that is the raising up and transformation into a Spirit-Body to continue to live in Spirit with eternal life. This is His Word that He taught me about the Testimony of my GOD the Father, and HIS Word is the Truth.

I have been sanctified by believing the Word of Truth to receive the Holy Spirit and the Spirit of my Lord Jesus Christ as I continue to follow His commands to keep myself sanctified with salvation, and that is how I deserve Him to live in Complete Unity within me. And I suffer to keep it that way every day of my life. I am filled with the Holy Spirit and the Spirit of my Lord Jesus Christ every moment of my life, and I will be led by them to know all the Word of Truth of this condemned Earthly Realm, which is transitory, and the Superior Eternal Spiritual Realm, which is my home.

Having this knowledge while living in the Spirit creates the inspiration for eternal life in me to mature in Spiritual Enlightenment for a higher level of truth in Spirit knowledge and for the eternal life that I have been gifted with by my Lord Jesus Christ since I was inspired by Him in receiving the Chrism of the Child.

Chapter 13 - Knowing When

Just about the time I turned sixty years old, I found myself at another crossroads to figure out where my life was going. There were a bunch of changes happening in the state department that I worked for. There were plans to reduce the number of facilities and staff support. It was a rumor for about a year until I got a message from an exceptionally reliable source that we were going to be disrupted from our work positions by job changes. No one knew exactly when or how it was going to happen. Most likely, it was going to be a demoralizing and chaotic process for most employees who would suddenly be affected. During these situations, it's like finding out who your true friends are when it is time to move all your belongings from one house to another across town, and everyone goes into hiding from you.

Since we sold our house, as we were guided to do by the Holy Spirit, we were living in a rental house for three years before the rumors began to manifest into our reality and the job changes took effect. So we started packing our things in boxes to make it easier for us, just in case we were suddenly guided to move again. To keep up with the Holy Spirit, we must listen for the foreknowledge that is given to us in signs, dreams, visions, etc. Our Lord Jesus Christ provides our direction for us to follow through the Holy Spirit in one way or another. As a Child of GOD, it's essential for me to be aware of the signs by listening for the whispers as I keep my mind sober to hear or see what is being revealed to me through my mind, heart, and Spirit. By praying in the Spirit, the thoughts will flow from my mind and descend into my heart for me to know by feeling that what is being said to me is true knowledge from my Lord Jesus Christ, and that comes through the Holy Spirit, who is my guide.

My Lord Jesus Christ told me that He would be with me for the rest of my life, and He has never failed me. I have only failed myself by my ignorance of the truth until I turned to Him repeatedly throughout my life for the correction of my own foolishness. And then I had to learn to remember to follow the commands that He has taught me, along with the visions that He has put in me to strengthen my Spirit with His own Spirit of Life. I learned that my life is a refining process that I must endure and master by keeping up with the guidance of the Holy Spirit.

Our life is like no other creation, and we are all made so uniquely different that no one can live our lives for us to achieve eternal life. Anything that we are gifted with through the Holy Spirit as a vision, vibration, symbol, sign, sound, dream, or Chrism in Spirit is tailored specifically for our individual Spirit to decipher the truth of it, so that we may mature in Spirit. Only by experiencing those gifts can we know them enough to understand them, and that is how we learn to have them in our heart, soul, and mind, living in the Spirit the self-control we need to firmly remain in Complete Unity, which is the point of perfection that we achieve living with our Lord Jesus Christ. His Spirit is living as One with mine: the one that I was first created with when it was put in my body. He is the Incorruptible Word of GOD that refills my depleted Spirit when it becomes weak, so I may become incorruptible by having Him in me with His Incorruptibility in me. And that is why no one can enter the Kingdom of GOD without taking part in my Lord Jesus Christ now. We need His Eternal Life and His Incorruptibility in us as One with our own personal Spirit. That is the way we are recreated a second time, reborn in Spirit, to become completely alive eternally by the Spirit of Life. This is how I live my life now: by taking part in Him as I live as One with Him. Everyone who believes in Him knows this: that He is the Way, the Truth, and the Life that we must remain attached to forever.

There are still things I must do that will be revealed to me throughout time, and I know He will lead me to the full knowledge of the truth. He always has and always will through the Holy Spirit. And I am telling everyone I can for them to know that He is the Word of GOD, and that He speaks in all languages, symbols, signs, sounds, vibrations, dreams, visions, and thoughts through the Holy Spirit for us to understand the Truth in the Word. When He speaks to me through the Holy

VINCENTE GARCIA

Spirit, He can trigger my mind to have the foreknowledge of my own future in the fraction of a second, no matter how much information it is. And it cannot be forgotten by me because it becomes burned into the memory of the mind. Think of it in the terms of a Spiritual upgrade that is alive in you, which inspires all the senses that can last forever in the mind and be hidden in your memory, until it is time to be recalled as fresh as the moment it was first experienced. It will only be revealed at the time it is needed to be believed in, as it becomes miraculously manifested in this Realm of Matter as another part of your life. This is how my faith becomes incorruptible by these little miracles I experience from time to time when I am reminded of who I am, not because I forget, but because I'm being loved in Spirit. That is a Spiritual language that we can learn from if we live in the Spirit now, as we are able to live in the Spirit Realm now with my Lord Jesus Christ. What is done in Heaven must be done on this Earth also.

As Child of Light, I had to set aside my own logical way of thinking that I learned from this Earthly Realm and pay attention to my Lord Jesus Christ speaking to me through the Holy Spirit from the Spirit Realm, which is the superior language that exists in every possible way. This Earthly Realm is an inferior reflection of the Spirit Realm, where the Chosen Ones are becoming enlightened to escape the condemnation of this world and the way of error, to then be moved to the Spirit

Realm of perfection, which is where our home is. The Spirit Realm is eternal for eternal life, while this Earthly Realm will pass away at the appointed time for its destruction.

A Spiritual message received may be beyond immediate comprehension for some people because they don't yet fully understand the meaning of the Spiritual language that they are learning for Spiritual Enlightenment, like most people who have a dream and wonder what it means. Keep in mind that a vision may be representing both realms of the Earthly and the Spirit Realm. That which is done on Earth is done in Heaven is how I live in the Spirit now. That is why I had to learn to cultivate patience in prayer and wait for the answers to be revealed to me for my understanding to become refined to perfection now, as I will be living in Heaven later after my Spiritual Transformation into a perfect Spirit-Body, as my Lord Jesus Christ is Spirit. Therefore, my Lord Jesus Christ taught me this about myself as He included Himself in this Word of Truth: that we can do nothing without our GOD the Father; we can only do what HE reveals to us which includes knowing when to do what HE shows us at the time HE wants us to do HIS will, and HE tells us when we are ready to do HIS will. He will always tell us when it is time to act. As Children of GOD, we are all living by HIS will when HE gives us the Words or Deeds to say or do through our Lord Jesus Christ by the guidance of HIS Holy Spirit that is within us, guiding our Spirit to act.

VINCENTE GARCIA

Anything is possible with GOD, including understanding the meaning of the word "believe." And especially now that HIS Son, who is my Lord Jesus Christ, has been given all the authority from my GOD the Father when He was glorified again in Heaven by our GOD the Father to do all things under the power of our GOD the Father. The question that remains is when should a person start believing? Remember this: there is no reason for anyone to be held back from believing in the Word of Truth, who is my Lord Jesus Christ, especially since we know that relying on logical reasoning cannot explain the secrets of the Spirit Realm anyway. He has revealed the Truth in the Word to us in many ways, and it is miraculous how He still does. I am living proof of that, and I know there are so many more who are being enlightened at this time. Because we are all gifted differently, we must mature into those gifts throughout our lives by experiencing a relationship with the Holy Spirit that leads us to the truth that we must each learn to accept naturally. It cannot be forced; we have to be made ready by accepting our Lord Jesus Christ and keeping His commands. We all have an infinite learning experience, unique from person to person, because of everyone's own unique Spirit creation from the time each person was first formed by our Lord Jesus Christ and recreated through the power of the Holy Spirit from our GOD the Father.

My Lord Jesus Christ is the only One begotten Son of GOD the Father. He is HIS Christ, who was anointed by my GOD the Father with Forethought, Foreknowledge, Eternal Life, Incorruptibility, and Truth in Him. Then He was glorified with the power of my GOD the Father at the time of His Spirit Creation with and by my GOD the Father, who allowed everything to be created through Him. Therefore, He asked our GOD the Father: Let us make man in our Image. That was a question and the will of our Lord Jesus Christ to do the will of our GOD the Father. That is how my Lord Jesus Christ taught me to ask of my GOD the Father by HIS will. I pray in Spirit, and I never say: Can you?, to my GOD the Father, when I know whatever I ask of HIM in the Name of HIS Son Jesus Christ, I ask to glorify HIM, at the same time I know that HE will do it as if it is already done. Because all power for creation comes from our GOD the Father and through our Lord Jesus Christ, the Firstborn and only Son that our GOD the Father manifested before Heaven and Earth was created through Him. My Lord Jesus Christ is loved by my GOD the Father, and He is teaching us to become like Himself to also be loved by my GOD the Father. So, if you want to be loved by our GOD the Father, learn to become like our Lord Jesus Christ by living with Him in Complete Unity as you keep His commands. Only those who live by loving my Lord Jesus Christ do so by keeping His commands, and only by doing His will do they also live with and by His eternal life as One.

VINCENTE GARCIA

Now that we were packed and ready to move at a moment's notice, after being prompted to act by foreknowledge of the changes that would be revealed to us later, we waited for the revelation to present itself through the Holy Spirit. Our personal belief with each other is that, as a married couple living joined in the Bridal Chamber within our Body-Temple as One, we must both agree with two yes answers about anything, at any time, on any subject through the guidance of the Holy Spirit that we share with each other as One. And nothing ever overrides that commitment within us living in the Spirit.

We do not blaspheme against the Holy Spirit, as we both have Him living in us with all due respect for each other, always living in the Spirit. Anyone who denies the truth, spoken from a person who has the Chrism of the Holy Spirit, is guilty of blasphemy against the Holy Spirit that is from GOD HIMSELF and will not be forgiven on Earth or in Heaven. Children of GOD the Father must always respect the truth, living with the Holy Spirit.

We were both ready and patiently waiting for the sign to know when it was time to move. It became surreal to go to work at the place that I had dwelled for eight years, to then find myself looking around, thinking about everything I was used to seeing, and that this might be the last time I would see them. Then I started kind of saying goodbye to everyone and telling them what good friends they were to us, and how much we were going to miss seeing them. It's hard to do when it comes to you so suddenly. But that's part of life, and that's why we must make the very best of every moment of our lives with good people. We must take every opportunity to live our lives in love to the fullest, because we never know when it will suddenly end.

There is one thing that is guaranteed: we are seeing and experiencing the past in this Earthly Realm as all things are constantly changing and all things come to an end. By the time we know what we had just experienced it has already happened and it is gone forever. Our hope is not to be part of this world and its passing when it does. The Chosen Ones are recreated to become Resurrected in this world by living in the present with eternal life for our future as we live and die in the flesh to become Redeemed into the Spirit Realm of our future home to continue living with eternal life in the Kingdom of our GOD the Father.

It didn't take long for the message of knowing when it was revealed, which came as a bit of a surprise to me, how it happened. I was at work in my office one night, with the lights out in the housing unit while everyone was asleep. As I was looking at my computer, it just shut off and the computer monitor went blank as if it lost power. I thought it was a blackout power outage at first, until I noticed that the backup emergency ceiling light never turned on and everything else electronic was still on. All of a sudden, the computer monitor lit up, and the screen showed a little bit of a scrambled color background, then shut off and went blank again. I thought that the computer monitor was going to restart, but instead the monitor displayed static pixels with the words "IT'S TIME" displayed in two-inch letters perfectly clear over the static on the screen for just a split second and the vision of it burned into my memory. I looked away from the screen and could still see the words "IT'S TIME" floating around in my vision with my eyes open in the dark. If I were not focused intently on the static on the screen for that flash of a moment, I would have missed it. Those words immediately triggered thoughts in my mind that everything I have been waiting for all my life to know would soon be revealed to me, and that it was time for me to retire so I could start ministering to my GOD the Father and my Lord Jesus Christ.

I was astonished and enlightened again at the same time, and I must have sounded like I found a fortune when I called my wife to tell her the news of what had just happened. She immediately agreed and said, "That's amazing, let's go." That made the feeling in me all that much better and more enlightening because she was also waiting to know when it was time to go.

I had just finished my fifteen-year plan of working for the department, and we had been living with just the basic essentials in the house that would fit into one truck. So, we were already prepared to go as we were told in advance to be ready. One thought running through my head was that I was about to become "that guy" when I once said in an asking way, "I want to be that guy?" about sixteen years earlier, when my coworker told me his father retired from the department after fifteen years of service and spent his life traveling the world with his wife.

I also couldn't help but notice that my Lord Jesus Christ had given me a sign and symbol by communicating this message through my sight by utilizing a computer monitor to let me know when it was time to minister to Him. That was a first for me, and it made me happy to remember that nothing is impossible with the power of my GOD the Father. Now I had confirmation that everything created in this material Realm of Matter is always in play for us to learn from. This was nothing short of what I call a little miracle created just for me to see in a flash of a moment, without having to think about it when it happened, I just knew with my entire being. I only needed to keep the memory in my mind of what I had prayed for in Spirit to have the faith, power, patience, and self-control to recognize when I was being led to the truth that my prayer in Spirit was being manifested in this Earthly Realm of Matter. I am living in the present and in the future of what I was given as a vision from the past to lead me to the Truth. This kind of little miracle is how I know that I am living my past visions of my future in my present time, so I experience living in the past, present, and future all at the same time. I live to master my present life by what I was told was going to happen by the Holy Spirit. I work to live perfectly in the present, for my future by the will of GOD at all times through HIS Son Jesus Christ and HIS Holy Spirit who guides my Spirit. This is knowing and understanding my Lord Jesus Christ: that I am living in the Spirit that enlightens me with the inspiration for eternal life.

One of the most beautiful things about these visions was I had someone to share them with, and she knew everything that I had told her in advance before they came true. I knew exactly what my Lord Jesus Christ did through the Holy Spirit as a sign for me to know He is with me. Because I know nothing is impossible for my GOD the Father who knows the heart of HIS Chosen One that HE has given to my Lord Jesus Christ. I am HIS Child of Light and HE knows that I live my life doing nothing in word or deed except as what HE wants me to say and do by HIS will and mine.

Every day I praise and worship my GOD the Father by giving thanks to HIM through HIS Son, and in the Name of HIS Son my Lord Jesus Christ for helping me in every way to know when to act and do the will of my GOD the Father to glorify HIM. As I have learned from my Lord Jesus Christ, only our GOD the Father knows the day and time for everything I must do and say in my life. Therefore, I will continue to live and wait with patience forever through my Lord Jesus Christ and for my GOD

KNOWING WHEN

the Father to let me know when it is HIS will for me to know HIS will, and when it is time by HIS time.

Chapter 14 - Clearing The Path

There are many religions that have been followed by people throughout history since the beginning of humanity on earth. Many of these have been forgotten, hidden, lost, or destroyed. I see all the written scriptures from the past religious teachers and prophets as history books from ancient civilizations that give us a description of what they may have imagined or have been shown by our GOD the Father what the power of the Spirit Realm would become in their future. Some of those hints fit into what I have learned to know is the Spiritual Word of Truth with details which only recently have been discovered to bring clarity to the mind for understanding and enlightenment by the knowledge which has been revealed to us in this day and age.

I have to take into consideration that the mindset from the influence of the worshippers of false gods in those days would cause the worship of the True Living GOD to become corrupted by politics for the control over the people, not allowing for the truth to be widely accepted and spoken without censorship or punishment up to and including death by the ruling powers over the people of those times.

Therefore, it is imperative to keep the Word of Truth spoken by my Lord Jesus Christ in my heart and safe in my mind to look at all scripture that I contemplate on for the consistency of what He has taught me to be the truth. There is no politics in the Word of Truth, only the truth given by the will of GOD that we must learn from HIS Son, our Lord Jesus Christ. With His words to help me, I succeed; without His word, I would fail.

It is evil to restrict the Spiritual worship that Christians must do to mature in Spirit, which is the honoring of my living GOD the Father of all creation, through HIS Son my Lord Jesus Christ at the will of HIS chosen people. Now that HE has given us a New Covenant of the Spirit through HIS Son, my Lord Jesus Christ, any kind of restrictions for worshipping HIM through my Lord Jesus Christ according to the New Covenant as we are required to do in this day and age are now called Antichrist. Therefore, any censorship against the free and open speech of my GOD and HIS Son Jesus Christ my Lord is a violation of my entire existence because I am One with them in my Spirit living in Complete Unity, which compels me to speak with everyone that wants to know them.

As a Chosen Spiritual One, this is who I am recreated me in Spirit to become: perfect in Spirit, in this Earthly Realm to begin living my Spiritual eternal life now. Immediately after the death of my Body-Temple, is when the promised Redemption will take effect where I am transformed into a perfect Spirit-Body to live on the created New World in the Spirit Realm, where all things are created new, to last forever without sin or death.

Religious books are not alive or magical, nor is one set higher than another. Some are called holy because they were brought forth by holy people who were inspired by the knowledge of my Living GOD the Father. I have been led to know the Truth in the Spirit of my Lord Jesus Christ, so that I can recognize what has been inspired to be written consistently by every person who has ever written the original concept of the Word of Truth throughout time. But the only one of all those that never sinned and died in the flesh without sin is my Lord Jesus Christ. So, I will only believe in what He has taught me to be the standard for every word that was written in any other scripture since the beginning of the world. By that standard, I keep His commands and will continue to show that I love Him.

I would like to think that all books are good things to bring us wisdom and knowledge to become closer to the love of GOD, but that is the farthest thing from the truth. There were religious and political leaders throughout time that have manipulated the translations of the Truth in the Word of GOD to fit their own church doctrines; to forge an agenda to intentionally misrepresent and distract the multitudes of people to keep them from having the Keys to enter the Kingdom of GOD which is within the reach of each and every one of us to live Spiritually perfect with my

VINCENTE GARCIA

Lord Jesus Christ now in the Kingdom of Heaven within us.

To help me clear this path from confusion as a Chosen Spiritual One, I was taught to understand Spiritual knowledge having received the Chrism of the Child at a very young age, and that I was not recreated to follow any doctrine made by mankind because they are repulsive to the Holy Spirit in me. I was recreated to follow the Holy Spirit of my Living GOD the Father within me, as my Lord Jesus Christ taught me how to live in the Spirit of the New Covenant from our GOD the Father. I paid attention to my Lord Jesus Christ to overcome fear and doubt as I accepted Him without hesitation before I knew what the bible books were. He told me that I was made to follow the will of my GOD the Father.

The evil spirits in this world have confused the minds of man with words, to make what is good words seem bad, and what is bad words seem good. So we must be careful with the words that we use that come out of our mouth. Corrupted speech is the demonic way to keep people confused and the truth hidden from them. We are held accountable for every word that comes out of our mouths, and we must repent our mistakes. My desire is not my will, because will is pure, perfect, and superior over my desire. Desire is of the flesh to exist only as it is made in this inferior Earthly Realm, and the will of my GOD the Father has become my will in Spirit, which is from HIM in the real Superior Spirit Realm.

CLEARING THE PATH

Therefore, living in Complete Unity in Spirit now is living as I was born, I am reborn, and I will be reformed forever after my death of my Body-Temple and my redemption into my Spirit-Body to continue to live an incorruptible eternal life in the Heavenly Spirit Realm.

I knew how to be filled with His Spirit and the Holy Spirit since childhood to not be subject to the confusion of sacrilegious doctrines within this world, but to instead have been given my sanctification and salvation from my Lord Jesus Christ in the language of the Spirit Realm at the Chrism of the Child that was given to me. The same Chrism that we all have the ability to accept at any time in our lives right now as Children of GOD the Father, living in Spirit for HIM through our Lord Jesus Christ, HIS first and only begotten Son.

If a person does not receive Complete Unity now as the living dead to become the living alive, they cannot receive it later; as the living dead dies they cannot receive the Chrism of Life. The living dead must receive the Resurrection in the flesh now to become the living alive; they cannot receive it later after death. When the living dead die, without receiving my Lord Jesus Christ, they cannot receive the Chrism of Life. The living dead must receive the Chrism of the Child to receive Life from my Lord Jesus Christ and to have the Resurrection now to pass over from living in death and condemnation to living alive in salvation, which is living within the Light of Life, that is my Lord Jesus Christ. He is truly living alive in me now. Therefore, those that are living alive with the Light of Life now die alive and will continue to receive eternal life by the promised Redemption to have eternal life after being raised by the Holy Spirit that is given to us from our GOD the Father through HIS Son, our Lord Jesus Christ.

There are many that call on my Lord Jesus Christ with the desire to be saved, but that is not enough when they fall short for salvation because they do not have the will to follow through with their commitment to live their lives with Him to know Him, by keeping His commands which is the only way to prove they love Him.

The path has been cleared by my Lord Jesus Christ at the time of His death and Resurrection on the Cross by the Holy Spirit of my GOD the Father. Now He has been given the authority to send us the Holy Spirit to be guided to the truth as my Lord Jesus Christ is also with us in Spirit as One. We don't have to wait for our Body-Temple to die before we know we have salvation in Him. By knowing this, you know the time to receive Him is now in order to have the symbol of the Cross by accepting His Chrism of the Holy Spirit to become Resurrected to eternal life with Him in Complete Unity. He is the Word, Truth, and the Way to Eternal Life. This is the Word of Truth, and nothing can hold us from having sanctification and salvation to live in perfect eternal life with Him; unless by our own lack of decision by not deciding to accept Him, as I have learned to accept Him with all my heart, mind, and Spirit with all the love I have. And He has taught me how to explain these things in the Spiritual Word of Truth for others to know Him and accept Him because there is no longer any excuse for anyone not to accept Him and my GOD the Father who created and sent Him. No one judges you because it is your own decision if you refuse the gift of eternal life and stay as you are condemned to the Second Death of your own Spirit, or it is your own decision to accept the gift of eternal life for the Second Creation of your Spirit to become recreated by the Resurrection in the Spirit of Complete Unity with our Lord Jesus Christ.

Do not limit yourself from accepting the Spirit of our Lord Jesus Christ which is a gift of freedom from living with the insanity of this Realm. If you are alive and breathing, you are worthy of being released from the condemnation of sin in this world to live perfectly in mind, body, and Spirit that is capable of becoming perfect and free of all sin by learning how to have our Lord Jesus Christ protecting you from sin and evil the very second you believe in His powerful glory to live within you. Clear your heart, mind, and Spirit to accept our Lord Jesus Christ within you and follow His commands by being led by the Holy Spirit of our GOD the Father, in Complete Unity to remain a Child of Light living in the Spirit right now and forever.

VINCENTE GARCIA

Bring yourself forth into the Living Light of my Lord Jesus Christ with all your sin and reject the evil within yourself by praying through my Lord Jesus Christ to ask my GOD the Father for forgiveness to become sanctified and without sin. Ask in Spirit prayer, and it shall be done if you ask without any fear or doubt to believe it will be done. The darkness of evil and sin cannot live in the light of my Lord Jesus Christ within you. The sin and evil that is hidden in darkness within you will flee or die when it is brought out into the power of the Living Light of my Lord Jesus Christ. When you have the Living Light of my Lord Jesus Christ within you, and you are in His Light as One, you become hidden in Him, and His Living Light within you is your superior salvation and protection from evil forever: that is where you cannot be seen or touched by evil one's ever again as long as you remain faithful in keeping His commands.

There are religious books for evil people to follow demons as their gods, which is a foolish thought to those who are enlightened by the Spirit of my living GOD the Father through HIS Son, my Lord Jesus Christ. Because living with demons will lead to the same condemnation and destruction of the spirit they are waiting to receive. Only the religious books that were written about the testimony of my GOD, HIS Holy Spirit, and HIS only begotten Son, my Lord Jesus Christ, are a useful source to confirm our understanding and knowledge by how those people described their interactions between the Holy Spirit and themselves. I like to know those things and read what they have recorded even if some of them are inaccurate or miss the mark on a few translations. I know that as long as I ask for the truth in Spirit prayer, I will be led to the truth in the Word of Truth to remain consistent in living in it.

In my search and comparisons of the books, I look for what has been consistently written over time throughout all the scriptures in the books, and then contemplate on those specific things to mature in the Word of Truth. And if my GOD the Creator is at the center of attention, there will also be the Son of GOD created by my GOD the Father. And the only Son of GOD was anointed with the Nature of the Spirit of our GOD the Father. Then HE Named HIS Son Jesus Christ, who fulfills all things with what was put in Him at His Chrism by our GOD the Father. And the Son, my Lord Jesus Christ, who was with my GOD the Father, has been witnessed in this Earthly Realm in the perfect flesh and Spirit, to show us the Nature of GOD the Father, who is perfect love. GOD is love, and HE created HIS Son with the same perfect nature of love. And the Holy Spirit of our GOD the Father, that comes out of our GOD the Father, is also put in our Lord Jesus Christ which makes them One, is also put in us to make us One with them in Complete Unity, as my Lord Jesus Christ prayed for us to become One with them on the day He was put on the crucifix to die.

VINCENTE GARCIA

When we receive the Holy Spirit from our GOD the Father, we are One with HIM and HIS Holy Spirit who guides us, and we also receive the Spirit of HIS Son, our Lord Jesus Christ, to also become One with Him with our Spirit. Therefore, the Spirit of GOD, the Spirit of Jesus Christ, the Holy Spirit of GOD, and our Spirit become One in Spirit. That makes us the fourth Spirit in the Kingdom of Heaven as One within us. As my Lord Jesus Christ taught me: The Kingdom of Heaven is within us, and blessed is the person who sees themself as the fourth One in the Kingdom of Heaven. The Holy Spirit does not make us their equal; He makes us functional with them, and of course, we are unique in our own Spirit recreation. We do not create; we are the created and we are recreated in Spirit. This fact has been disputed in every way and now stands indisputable by the witnesses who have written thousands of texts, letters, and books for several countries. They were retranslated into many languages and dialects throughout time to span the world, and there is overwhelming evidence that proves my Lord Jesus Christ has risen from death and was seen alive after His resurrection from the crucifix. He was once put to death on the crucifix to die once for all of mankind to have salvation, if they so decide to accept His gift of life that was put in Him by our GOD the Father.

I proclaim that I am a Chosen Spiritual One, and that my Lord Jesus Christ chose me to become a Child of

Light to do His will today and to explain my Chrism of the Child in these writings, which is also the will of my GOD the Father whom I serve through my Lord Jesus Christ who tells me what I need to know through the Holy Spirit that is with my Spirit and guiding me with the Living Spirit Light of Power. I proclaim that my Lord Jesus Christ has been given the authority over all things to give His Eternal Life to whoever keeps His commands and accepts His help to become One with Him in Spirit without any fear or doubt.

Original writings and copies of scripture were written as letters to others without numbered sentences or verses as we use today for reference. They are regular letters or laws written to convey the important messages for the people of those days to reach a higher level of understanding by experiencing the power of inspiration within us. When I began to read the bible scriptures for myself, I found the numbers to be annoying to read around. Some people can memorize the words and verse numbers to recite them. That is a talent that is commendable, but it is of little use when it comes to becoming enlightened by the truth if the meanings are not understood and put into practice for internal inspiration. If reading is all you have to do to become sanctified for salvation, then everyone who has read the scriptures would believe in our Lord Jesus Christ and follow His commands like their eternal life depended on it for salvation as a start.

VINCENTE GARCIA

Knowing the truth by contemplating on the Word of Truth sanctifies our mind, and by accepting the truth inwardly into our heart and Spirit, we may become sanctified to express the truth outwardly from the heart where our belief comes from. We must cleanse the inside of our cup, because everything that comes out of a person comes from the heart, and if that which is in the heart is purified with the truth, then nothing corrupting can come forth out of the person's mouth except the perfect truth.

Therefore, firstly knowing the scriptures is the basic beginning that paints the picture of events in our minds as we begin to believe the truth correctly. The second basic step is to understand the true interpretations of the scriptures to gain knowledge of what is written in the Gospel of my Lord Jesus Christ, to understand how we must live in the Spirit by keeping His commands in our hearts. The third basic step is to become compelled by our Spirit nature to act in support of our belief and understanding, which readies us by our faith to accept our Spiritual and physical transformation so that we may endure living our life by knowing what our GOD the Father is asking of us every moment of our lives. Finally, the fourth is asking to be forgiven for all of our own sin for salvation, by committing ourselves in Spirit prayer to our GOD the Father in the Name of HIS Son Jesus Christ for the Chrism of receiving HIS Holy Spirit and the Spirit of our Lord Jesus Christ in Complete Unity, and to lead our life under HIS New

Covenant of the Spirit with the New Command to always love each other.

That is the time when your life of living in the flesh with condemnation ends, and your new eternal life of living in the Spirit begins. You can't find the beginning of your new life in the Spirit until you find the end of your old life in the flesh. That is the crossing over from death to life. At that time, with the help of our Lord Jesus Christ, we turn from the weak desire of the flesh towards the strong will of the Spirit. That is the recreation, a second Spiritual creation of our birth in the Body-Temple Bridal Chamber, where our Spirit becomes One with the Holy Spirit of our GOD that will be with us and lead us to the truth, with the Spirit of our GOD the Father, and with the Spirit of HIS Son our Lord Jesus Christ, in Complete Unity for eternal life by receiving our own Resurrection from the Oil of the Cross, which is the Chrism of the Spirit, the anointing of our Spirit. Our faith, living with the Holy Spirit, is for receiving Him who is the gift of eternal life; and our love that we have living in Spirit, is for helping to give the gift of life to each other as we love one another.

This is the knowledge that I was taught by my Lord Jesus Christ to have the understanding of living in the Spirit. There are four things that I must remember in my mind, heart, and Spirit to live in the Spirit. These are for understanding and having knowledge in the mind, body and Spirit that we must receive the Holy Spirit, the

VINCENTE GARCIA

Enlightenment, the Cross, and the Resurrection. At the time we receive our Lord Jesus Christ, we are resurrected within our Body-Temple and remain that way until after our Body-Temple dies and we are redeemed and transformed into a Spirit-Body like our Lord Jesus Christ is at this time. This is the language of the Holy Spirit of Light that speaks to us in signs, symbols, sounds, dreams, visions, and vibrations. Those who will live in the Spirit must learn to hear and see in the Spirit without any doubt or fear.

Following the Word of Truth is to become enlightened and glorified by the Spirit of GOD through my Lord Jesus Christ. HIS living Word of Life is HIS Son Jesus Christ, HIS Choice, HIS Chrism, HIS Anointed, HIS Word, HIS Christ, HIS Living Light, HIS Covenant of the Spirit, and HIS gift for us is to accept Him by the decision of our own free will out of our love for our GOD the Father in the Name of HIS Son, our Lord Jesus Christ.

As a Chosen Spiritual One, I continuously become filled up in Spirit as One in Complete Unity with the Holy Spirit that my Lord Jesus Christ sends into my Spirit. Our Body-Temple is like a Spiritual cup that holds our Spirit and must be cleaned on the outside and also on the inside before we are filled up with the Holy Spirit and the Spirit of my Lord Jesus Christ. Those who do not learn how to live this way with the Spirit of our Lord Jesus Christ through the Holy Spirit every day and moment of their lives will remain condemned as they already are, without the possibility of having life because they live without His help. Only by having our Lord Jesus Christ will we ever be with our GOD the Father for eternal life starting now, in this day and age, and later after we are instantly redeemed and transformed into Spiritual Beings like our Lord Jesus Christ was redeemed to enter the Kingdom of GOD. Those who are ready now are ready to go at any time.

For over fifty-five years, I have kept an open mind to learn and understand why I was chosen to be led on my own path to receive the Chrism of the Child, which is the Chrism of the Holy Spirit placed into me by my Lord Jesus Christ for my Resurrection, at a very young age. Although it has been a blessing and a mystery to me, I consider myself fortunate to have been made a Chosen Spiritual One destined to skip the corruption of false interpretations, church doctrine, idol traps, blindfolds, burdens, lies, and perverted practices, before I understood how to accept the truth in the power of my Lord Jesus Christ within me. And still, I am not exempt from bearing my own cross and enduring anything the world tempts me with.

I understand that the blessing of the power from my GOD the Father is constantly flowing through my Lord Jesus Christ into me by the Holy Spirit that is within me forever. Therefore, my faith in my GOD and HIS Son is essentially irreversible through my understanding the

Word of Truth that I have experienced in many ways on my Spiritual path.

That is why when I stepped into a church at a young age for the first time, as the Holy Spirit compelled me to, I didn't go there to repent or to be saved for myself in the traditional sense of the word "saved." Those thoughts never crossed my mind at that time because it did not exist in my childhood as something necessary to be learned from textbooks, or a preacher from a local church. I now know that I was fortunate to have never watched television before the time I was introduced to the power of my Lord Jesus Christ in the Spirit Realm. Television can become a distraction for children as multimedia can be a distraction for adults too. I accepted Him into my heart, mind, and Spirit by naturally experiencing His presence in my own life as a child without any doubt. I welcomed Him in my life and I always look for Him to speak to me again. My thoughts at that time were that everyone was hearing and seeing images of the Spirit Realm for themselves to know my Lord Jesus Christ like I did. To me, that had to be why they knew His Name. Only, I didn't understand why they didn't want to talk about it.

So, I went to the local church compelled by the will to sing praises to honor my Lord Jesus Christ with all the love I had in my entire being. I had nothing else to give because I had already given HIM everything I had: myself. And I already accepted to be One with Him –

inside and outside as One – anytime He spoke to me. That is how I learned to be as One with him: by practicing how to communicate with Him in Spiritual telepathy like a Spiritual prayer with visions.

All this happened before I ever owned a bible or read a single verse because I believed in my Lord Jesus Christ with all my existence without doubting or having fear within me because He is with me forever. I have no reason to believe otherwise because He has proven to me that He is living within me. The only thing that matters in this realm of the flesh is to live in Spirit, knowing my GOD the Father and HIS Son Jesus Christ with everything I am, and to be One with them in Complete Unity, inside and out. That is why He shows Himself to me, and I believe He has shown Himself to others who have learned to listen to Him through the Holy Spirit in signs, sounds, symbols, dreams, vibrations, and visions. Like the little miracles that I have been given all these years. I cannot unsee what I have been given to see and experience in the Spirit Realm, where time doesn't exist the same as it does in this Earthly Realm of Matter. Knowing what it is like to be living alive and enlightened in the Spirit brought me to the awareness of those who are still condemned and living dead, trapped within their flesh with the insanity that they have no future after death. My Lord Jesus Christ freed me from being trapped in the flesh with insanity.

VINCENTE GARCIA

I also know the truth by the testimony of others, being that they have been shown things in the same way that I myself have seen Spirits. One person I met watched a demon step out of himself when he received our Lord Jesus Christ and was saved. He needed to see that to bring his level of faith, power, patience, and self-control up, and no one will ever change his mind from going to our Lord Jesus Christ ever again. We become humble, loving, and cleansed from sin by keeping His commands and following the guidance of the Holy Spirit. We do it without any fear or doubt in Spiritual prayer to our GOD the Father in the Name of our Lord Jesus Christ. Whether we are alone or together as brothers and sisters, we are One in our Lord Jesus Christ.

These Chosen Ones are my brothers and sisters living in the Body of Jesus Christ, which is the true Church. They do not do anything or say anything without checking in with our GOD the Father in order to do HIS will in the Name of our Lord Jesus Christ, HIS Son. Take the path of your guide, the Holy Spirit who leads you to the truth. If you do not follow Him, you will not be forgiven for the blasphemy of calling Him a liar through your actions of denying yourself to live in the Word of Truth with the Holy Spirit and our Lord, Jesus Christ. I only hope this truth is understood by all who read it and receive it in the Name of our Lord Jesus Christ for eternal life.

CLEARING THE PATH

As a Chosen One, I had to endure my own refining on my own Spiritual path that I must continue to endure. Even when I had fallen into my weaknesses, I learned to turn for help and guidance from the Holy Spirit while learning from my own experiences. And because my belief could not be broken, I had to learn to reset my life quickly by turning back to the help of my Lord Jesus Christ, who is my eternal life. He helps me clear my path to righteousness by reminding me to remain in His love. Without humbling myself and doing that, I would have remained in condemnation, which would result in my own shame, judgement, to result in my own doom and destruction. I am not exempt from enduring and winning the contest to overcome my sufferings in this world while being anointed by the Oil of the Cross, inspired by the Holy Spirit, Enlightened by knowledge of the truth, and resurrected for eternal life at this time. I must bear it in faith, power, self-control, and patience that the Holy Spirit gives me. I embrace it to receive my portion of eternal life from my Lord Jesus Christ, as He has commanded me to keep His commands, to know how to show my love for Him.

Like all others, I must also be refined, like the ore of gold is refined, from a dirty mixture of the worldly things and into the purified Light of Life living in the Spirit. I must keep in mind that I am constantly being refined and there is no end to the renewing of my Spirit with the power in the Holy Spirit of my GOD the Father through my Lord Jesus Christ. The Life of the Holy Spirit never sleeps within me and is constantly searching for ways to bring me closer to Spiritual perfection by keeping me holy in my heart, mind, and Spirit as I walk on my Spiritual path. As my Lord Jesus Christ has warned me, I cannot do this alone, and I cannot do this without having His help washing me clean from sin. I must become like my Teacher to always be learning more ways to bring glory to my GOD the Father and to please HIM.

It is my responsibility as a Chosen Spiritual One to be here helping others clear their paths because I know the Way, the Truth, and the Life because I am living in my Lord Jesus Christ as He is living in me. I am responsible for the blood of everyone in this corrupted world that is being called to my GOD the Father as if their blood is my own. If any of them is lost by the works of my hand allowing them to be led astray, then I will lose my own eternal life. If any of them ask me to walk with them on their path for a mile, I am willing to go with them forever until I am led away to help another. I am my brothers' and my sisters' keeper, and they are mine. They bring me the most happiness when I hear they are diligently pursuing the Word of Truth, having my Lord Jesus Christ living with them in Complete Unity.

Some people are so close to becoming enlightened that it's just like they are standing on the path to righteousness and may walk off of it because they don't recognize it. That's for not having cared for their path, so it became covered over with the dirt of this world that blinds them from seeing the true path of the Spirit. My path was set in place before me from before the time I was born, but it's a matter of effort on my part to decide to do the righteous things and accept the gift of life from my GOD the Father. I live to prove that I have the will to remain worthy of HIM living in Spirit by my faith and I must keep the commands that HE passed on to me through my Lord Jesus Christ.

One of the greatest lies that false prophets and evil doers have passed down through the ages is that we must fear God. That is an old expression that is misinterpreted by misunderstanding of the scripture. It twists the truth and keeps people in those chains of fear that will keep them from going to HIM. By that, I know that subtle expression is used to make people believe they can never be worthy of salvation, because they have been falsely taught that they are not worthy of my Lord Jesus Christ because they have sinned. I not only have been given enlightenment by the truth, but I have also been given enlightenment by understanding the questions that lead to the answers in the Truth. The question remains in the Word of Truth, "If I am not worthy of my Lord Jesus Christ, then why did He die for me?" To believe in Him is to believe in the power of the salvation in His death for me that He gave me to have eternal life because He believes that I am worthy, and I believe Him with all my heart, mind, and Spirit that I am worthy by His choosing me. If there wasn't any unrighteous person on earth that could be saved, He would not have come down to this Earthly Realm at all. I have made the decision to accept that fact as I have accepted His Spirit to be One in Complete Unity with my Spirit. I am the fourth Spirit in the Kingdom of Heaven within me. I do not need anyone except Him showing me through the Holy Spirit, to help me believe that He showed the world that this is the Truth in the Word, and I believe Him without any doubt or fear. Doubt and fear are a lie, and my Lord Jesus Christ taught me to never doubt or fear. Therefore, I live in my Spirit with the love of my GOD the Father through my Lord Jesus Christ, following the guidance of HIS Holy Spirit in Complete Unity by HIS will without any doubt or fear.

The true meaning of the word "fear" in the scriptures can be better understood as, "do not disappoint our GOD the Father, and continue to show your love for HIM by resisting all evil." By doing this, it is impossible to fear HIM, as I have never feared my GOD the Father who loves me and gives me eternal life. How can anyone fear love, and my GOD the Father is pure love. To be consistent in the Word of Truth, we must replace fearing GOD with loving GOD as my Lord Jesus Christ has taught me to Love GOD with all my mind, heart, and spirit while living in the Spirit in Complete Unity with HIM. There is no fear in pure love.

The truth has always been that my GOD the Father is love and no one should ever fear love. If you fear love, then there is something that is very wrong with you, and most likely, you don't know what love is. Just think: if you could relive your life to know that you have no sin in you, wouldn't you feel ready and willing to go to our GOD the Father, to be presented to HIM clean and ready to be accepted in HIS presence and love? Of course you would. HE knows that, and HIS will is for that to be our life now. HE shows us by providing the Way for us through HIS Son Jesus Christ helping us. Accept HIS gift of life to have HIS Son in you, as it is the will of our GOD for you to become free from the filth of sin, and present yourself as a Holy Spiritual Child to HIM now. Stay busy and fix yourself through the help of our Lord Jesus Christ who will help you clear your path to our GOD the Father.

My Lord Jesus Christ tells me that I must keep His commands, and the greatest command is to love GOD with all my heart, mind, and soul in Spirit. He also commanded me to never fear. Therefore, as a Chosen One living with complete love for my GOD the Father, there is not the smallest speck of room for any fear to enter into the perfect love that I have for my Living GOD of Spirit. No one can change that; no one can touch that; it just is, and always will be my will to live by HIS will at all times.

VINCENTE GARCIA

As an enlightened Child of GOD, I will have love for my GOD the Father because HE loves me. And I have love for the Son of GOD, my Lord Jesus Christ, who sees me worthy to die for. My GOD the Father loves me by HIS will, and my Lord Jesus Christ loves me with His will, because it is the will of His GOD the Father, as they are living as One with me: One with my personal Spirit and HIS Holy Spirit in Complete Unity. This is part of knowing the clear path of the Chosen Spiritual One that lives by the will of GOD and the will of HIS Son, Jesus Christ.

One reason why our GOD the Father sent our Lord Jesus Christ is because so many people refused to go to HIM to believe in HIM out of their fear of HIS almighty power. People lived in fear of dying for not being able to keep HIS commands in the Old Covenant. So, our GOD the Father sent HIS only Son, our Lord Jesus Christ, who showed us all nothing but love as an example of how much love our GOD the Father has for us who are the descendants of Adam. By that lesson, I know that the plan for creation by my GOD the Father, has not changed. We are at the beginning of creation, and HIS will is for all to live eternal life as HE removes all error and evil from creation. That's the next step in creation, and the sooner we realize that we are part of that with the power in the Name of our Lord Jesus Christ to help ourselves and others, the sooner we can begin living in the Spirit with eternal life by the Resurrection within us.

Our Lord Jesus Christ also tells us that He will not ask our GOD the Father for the things we need to glorify HIM. Our Lord Jesus Christ made it clear that we must ask of HIM on our own because our GOD the Father loves us. Just do your asking in Spirit prayer with honor to GOD while honoring HIS Son, and asking in the Name of HIS Son, our Lord Jesus Christ, without any fear or doubt. By that, we acknowledge that we respect HIS Son so HE will give us what we need to glorify HIM. And asking in this way, we must live our lives as our prayers have been answered and as though we have already received what we asked for to glorify our GOD the Father because of our faith in HIM and HIS Son.

No one can glorify our GOD the Father without asking for all of their own sins to be forgiven first or before praying in the Spirit to HIM. If you turn from all sin by turning to our Lord Jesus Christ to be forgiven for your sin by our GOD the Father, you glorify HIM, and your prayers shall be answered in your favor. And they will love you and bless you and help you with everything you will ever need to give you eternal life now. For your redemption after your Body-Temple dies, you will be raised up into a Spirit-Body with eternal life.

Follow my Lord Jesus Christ because the Chosen Spiritual One you follow is the Chosen Spiritual One you will become. The path you follow is following in the truth, and a Chosen Spiritual One is living by the New Covenant of the Spirit. My Lord Jesus Christ has already started making everything new since the time of His life and death in this Earthly Realm. If a person is living by the flesh of sin, then they are not saved in Christ Jesus and by their actions. They are the corrupt walking dead that do nothing for salvation and remain condemned without my Lord Jesus Christ.

Here is the truth and examples of it. Those that reject my Lord Jesus Christ reject the Spirit of Life in Him in the Spirit Realm, and at the same time, remain dead in their flesh while living in this Earthly Realm, which will result in the Second Death of their spirit for remaining in condemnation when it doesn't have to be that way. That which is done on Earth is done in Heaven. Therefore, by staying in condemnation, a person dies twice: once with the body of flesh in this Earthly Realm, and the Second Death of their Spirit in the Spirit Realm by spirit destroying fire.

This is the knowledge in the Word of Truth that my Lord Jesus Christ has taught me to know: that He has fulfilled the Way to salvation for us as it is written in the scriptures. Humanity has now been created in the image of GOD twice: once with the Spirit formed in the flesh, and the second being recreated in the flesh and reformed in Spirit for Complete Unity within the Body-Temple Bridal Chamber, the Holy of Holies within us.

At first, when humanity was created with Spirit and put in the flesh, my GOD the Father gave us the first

Covenant in the Mosaic Law. That Law could not give us salvation but brought death from our transgressions living by it in the flesh. Therefore, humanity was falling short of the glory of my GOD the Father for not being able to keep all the laws. The Mosaic Law was made transitory until the New Covenant of the Spirit of my Lord Jesus Christ was fulfilled to give us eternal life.

At last, after my Lord Jesus Christ was sent by my GOD the Father to fulfill the prophecy in the scriptures, and He had been risen by the Holy Spirit of my GOD the Father from death on the Crucifix, humanity is being recreated in Complete Unity of the Spirit to live a Holy Life in Spirit by the second and New Covenant of the Spirit of HIS Son Jesus Christ. Only through my Lord Jesus Christ is humanity allowed to have another lasting creation living in the Spirit for my GOD the Father who gives us salvation and brings forth eternal life through HIS Son.

Therefore, my GOD the Father looks upon us with love, and by HIS grace makes us worthy through HIS Testimony concerning my Lord Jesus Christ. My GOD the Father, gave us eternal life in HIS only begotten Son, my Lord Jesus Christ, and whoever has HIS Son has eternal life. Whoever does not have the Son sent by my GOD the Father, does not have eternal life. No one, especially after they have received the Holy Spirit and the Spirit of my Lord Jesus Christ, can say they are not worthy of Him, or they would be living and believing a lie in sin through their actions for not believing in the power of my Lord Jesus Christ to forgive sins and give life to those who keep His commands.

Since the Chrism of the Child, I was created a second time to live in Spirit, in Complete Unity. Therefore, the first Old Covenant, the Mosaic Law of the flesh, becomes last, and the last New Covenant of the Spirit becomes first. This is what my Lord Jesus Christ has taught me about: the first shall be last and the last shall be first. In other words, He taught me that the first Old Covenant of the flesh is inferior, and the last New Covenant of the Spirit with my Lord Jesus Christ is Superior.

It is also the same, just as the first baptism in water was done as a sanctification for keeping the commands of my GOD the Father, to abstain from living in sin and evil. So is the last Chrism of receiving the Holy Spirit from my GOD the Father through HIS Son, my Lord Jesus Christ for salvation in Spirit is done last. Therefore, I am recreated a superior and perfect Spirit with my Resurrection by the will of my GOD the Father through HIS Son, my Lord Jesus Christ to live in Complete Unity.

To have eternal life, I must live in the final Covenant, the Covenant of the Spirit of my Lord Jesus Christ that my GOD the Father has made for humanity to have eternal life with HIS Son, my Lord Jesus Christ, through the time of my death of my flesh. I won't die because I am recreated Spirit of the Second Creation; only my flesh will die while my Spirit will be raised up by the Holy Spirit and instantly taken to my Lord Jesus Christ to continue to live eternal life. Our flesh is transitory for this Realm; I felt that way since I was five years old and I just didn't know how to explain it.

The superior New Covenant of the Spirit of my Lord Jesus Christ has been fulfilled at the time my Lord Jesus Christ was raised to life. It has been in effect since that time, and the Chosen Ones are living by the New Covenant of the Spirit because this is the time in which the New Covenant of the Spirit is in effect. In other words, we are living our history in the age of the New Covenant of the Spirit. Which is, our GOD the Father has given us eternal life, and that eternal life is in HIS Son Jesus Christ. Whoever has HIS Son Jesus Christ has eternal life. Or whoever does not have Jesus Christ, the Son who was sent by the will of His GOD, His Father and our Father, does not have eternal life.

This is the most important decision you will ever decide in your life. It is not a choice that you can make anytime you feel like it. It is not a choice you can make at all, or it would have been made by many before our Lord Jesus Christ died for our salvation to make it possible. It is a decision to accept the choice of HIS gift forever, as you give yourself up willingly and freely to the only Living GOD the Father, to accept HIS Son Jesus Christ as your Lord and Savior for the rest of your eternal life, as you learn to keep living by HIS commands to walk with guidance of the Holy Spirit. Stay on the Spirit path that He will walk with you.

The reason why this is not a choice is because you are already condemned to death for doing whatever you desire and not accepting to live by the New Covenant of the Spirit. So, in this Earthly Realm of matter, you do not have a choice. You have one decision: to accept the gift of eternal life by having our Lord Jesus Christ, who is the fulfillment of the New Covenant of the Spirit that gives you life. It is a miracle when our GOD the Father sends HIS Holy Spirit into you. You will feel it without a doubt, and you will feel the most love, happiness, and fulfillment from your Spirit becoming enlightened with theirs as One in Complete Unity. There will be no denying the difference that you know you have been glorified with the Holy Spirit. As I have explained before, it just is, and I just know it's true because I can feel the Spirit of Life with my Lord Jesus Christ living in me. Therefore, I am compelled by the Holy Spirit to praise and worship my GOD the Father in Spirit and in the Name of my Lord Jesus Christ HIS Son.

For example, when a gift is given, you do not get to choose it; someone chooses it for you. Your only thing to do is to gracefully accept it or remain as you are without it. Your gift from our GOD the Father is to have our Lord Jesus Christ by accepting Him to be One within you with the power of His Spirit of Eternal Life in Him that will be living in you. And loving Him by keeping His commands, our GOD the Father will love you. And He, as your gift of life, will send to you the Holy Spirit that comes out of our GOD the Father to be in you as One with your Spirit to guide you.

The Holy Spirit within us that our Lord Jesus Christ speaks to us through, speaks to our Spirit within our Bridal Chamber, which is the Holy of Holies of our Spirit living within our Body-Temple. He will be your guide and advocate for your eternal life, even at the time when you are raised up by Him to be presented with Him to our GOD the Father. He will show you your future as needed to help keep your faith powerful with self-control and patience living in the Word of Truth.

This is the clearing of the path which has been made for you and within you that leads to our GOD the Father through HIS Son Jesus Christ who is the Way, the Truth, and the Life. Every Chosen Spiritual One must endure for themselves and help others understand to do the same by following the guidance of the Holy Spirit from our GOD the Father, in the Name of HIS Son, our Lord Jesus Christ.

Chapter 15 - Seeking the Lost

I was about the age of sixty-one when I was helping many friends rekindle their faith in my Lord Jesus Christ by sending them daily devotionals. I realized that this message was becoming well-received by people who had little time in their busy lives for going to a church. They expressed their appreciation for helping them learn the truth that they knew had been missing from their lives. From time to time, I would hear a testimonial from someone with renewed faith who had been lost from straying off the path of righteousness, and how their family was coming together again and turning to my Lord Jesus Christ.

When I asked what it was that inspired them to become compelled to start living in the truth again, they would admit how hearing their favorite daily devotional brought uncontrollable tears to their eyes when they finally remembered the love of our Lord Jesus Christ that has been waiting for them to turn back to it for such a long time. It is not my work; I am the messenger, and it is the works of my Lord Jesus Christ and the Holy Spirit inspiring them by their own faith to receive them every day. They are my brothers and sisters who are finally understanding how to remember that they have always wanted to be committed to live in Unity with my Lord Jesus Christ. This is the Word of Truth, that without my Lord Jesus Christ, no one can truly live and be alive.

VINCENTE GARCIA

I had prayed in Spirit for the answer to a question. I asked Him to show me the Holy Scriptures that I may share with people to help them become spiritually inspired now. The answer was given to me in a vivid vision-dream with the stipulation that every word that I would write was only to be written in Spiritual prayer to my GOD the Father every day until it was revealed to me that the writing was completed. At that time, I had the power of the Holy Spirit leading me on a path that only a Chosen Spiritual One could walk without doubt or fear: to hear, understand, say, and do exactly what I was told and shown to do by Him.

As a Chosen One who follows my Lord Jesus Christ through the Holy Spirit in faith, I had no idea where this was going or to what extent and depth the message would become. I only knew that I was being led to write about the Apostle John, chapters thirteen through seventeen of his letters, and that I was going to be guided on what and how to write in my own words the way I had been raised to believe and remain living in the Spirit with my Lord Jesus Christ. This is the answer to what I had asked for from my GOD the Father, and it would take over a year in prayer to complete the answer as it was revealed to me in Spirit prayer every day. I was excited and enlightened to know that I was the Chosen Spiritual One made ready for this task.

As I began to write, at first I felt that it was hard for me to keep up with the Holy Spirit. As time went by, the hours seemed like minutes and the days seemed like a few hours. I seemed to be living in the Spirit Realm, where I would never seem to get tired of writing, sometimes for twenty-two hours straight. I remember the Holy Spirit would wake me up at five in the morning to quickly write something down to remember it later, and I would realize that it was what I had been shown in the vision dream as I gathered my thoughts on the subject. By knowing that, I would write until two or three o'clock the next morning. I literally lost track of time because time was not a factor after I began writing the Word of Truth in Spirit prayer. I know it was by the power of the Holy Spirit that I was able to write my first book: Inspiration for Your Eternal Life. I never had a clue that I was being refined to do that; it just happened by the power of my Lord Jesus Christ, in His way and on His time – not my own. He will take me to a higher level of understanding of the Word of Truth as long as I find time for Him. That's always in my Heart. He's refining me to become the person I will be in the Superior Spirit Realm by teaching me to believe that I am living here now and in the Spirit Realm for a little while. Life is short in the flesh compared to eternity living in the Spirit in Complete Unity within the Body-Temple before it dies. It is easy for me to accept living with my best Spirit friends, who are the Holy Spirit of my GOD the Father and the Spirit of my Lord Jesus Christ. With my Spirit, I'm set in their ways. As I learn about living in the Spirit in this world and the Spirit Realm, I am directly connected to HIM within the Bridal Chamber where HIS power flows from HIM, through HIS Son, through HIS Holy Spirit, and through my Spirit in my Body-Temple as I am physically in contact with this world doing HIS will. I know who I am recreated to become, and there is no other way to be that in reality without my Lord Jesus Christ helping me.

When I started writing, the daily devotionals were a paragraph each, then two paragraphs, then a page each. After a couple of months, the number of recipients grew towards forty people, and then a hundred. Then a question arose from the amount of writing each devotional was: how long was I going to continue to write? The answer was given to me in another vision-dream, and it would be revealed later that I had to write until the editor had been chosen. I didn't question how or when it was going to happen; I just continued writing as I waited patiently for the next Spiritual intervention to enlighten me on this Spiritual path. It reminds me of the dream-vision where I was flying through space uncontrollably until I remained calm and focused on the direction I was going without fear or doubt: two things that my Lord Jesus Christ has taught me not to do or say, because fear or doubt doesn't exist in the Spirit Realm while I'm living with Him in complete unity.

As time went on, I realized what I was being led to do by the Holy Spirit after I remembered how this all started.

It started when I was contemplating the Word of GOD and by feeling the compassion that my Lord Jesus Christ has for all His Chosen Spiritual Ones that are being called to our GOD the Father. Some were in prison in the State Prison system, and others were in prison in their busy lives, as both were living without the inspiration for eternal life.

My gift of the Holy Spirit was the ability to identify who was actively seeking the truth but not finding it. It was revealed to me that it wasn't because they lacked a way to find it; it was the fact that they lacked the way to recognize the truth when they were looking straight at it every day. When people are blinded by the corrupt system of this world, and don't see a way out, or may have forgotten the value in themselves if they ever recognized it at all, they don't know who they are or what they are. That made me a little more sad every day until I couldn't stand by and let it happen anymore.

I was given these gifts to live with, and I needed to find a way to share them with others because I was told to by my Lord Jesus Christ in a vision: that it's time. That meant sharing the Word of Truth as I have been refined to know it. I didn't know how I was going to do it; I only knew that it was a gift by His choice for me to accept. The last thing I needed to know was how I was supposed to accomplish this task to please my GOD the Father to fulfill what I had asked HIM for in Spirit prayer. It was revealed to me in a vision dream that I would bring the Word of Truth to the Prison Facility and share the prophecy with them in person as a guest speaker in front of an audience. So my faith in my GOD the Father, and my Lord Jesus Christ was in full measure as I waited for the Holy Spirit to guide me on the path to fulfill the prophecy.

The mindset of a Chosen Spiritual One is first to please my GOD the Father with all my heart, mind, and soul in Spirit prayer and in the Name of my Lord Jesus Christ. Since I do not make my own choices, I wait for my instructions through the Holy Spirit to accept the choices that have been made for me as I am instructed to carry them out. And this is where I put forward all the patience I have received with the power of faith and self-control that He gives me. With that, there comes a feeling of urgency to keep up with the Holy Spirit that creates a tireless physical power within me that allows me to accomplish everything I have been commanded to do by the inspiration of interacting with Him. That feeling is unique, as if I am being inspired to know what to do and being physically drafted toward the direction He wants me to go. It seems effortless at the time because the power of GOD the Father is flowing through me in control.

By understanding the Spiritual knowledge that my Lord Jesus Christ has enlightened me with, I learned there is the infinite freedom of love waiting in the Word of Truth for the Chosen Ones. I cannot continue to watch people remain imprisoned by lies. It is time to tell the truth and help free the Children of GOD from condemnation, and I am the Chosen Spiritual One who was made ready and capable to reveal the Key and Way to help bring every orphan and widow that I can find to my Lord Jesus Christ through the introduction of these written messages. My Lord Jesus Christ is the only one in existence who has the power to give the freedom of Eternal Life to anyone who turns to believe in Him and follows Him. There are many ways to get there from where you are because no one knows the Spiritual path you are destined to travel, but there is no other way to receive it except through Him. This is the Testimony of our living GOD the Father, and it is the Word of Truth.

As I was being led to author a book of inspiration titled: Inspiration For Your Eternal Life, I knew the purpose would be revealed to me, so I was extremely motivated to get it done as best as I could. I would wake up at five o'clock in the morning and write until two or three o'clock the next morning. I didn't keep track of time because I was in constant prayer as much as I could be to bring the truth in the Word of GOD to the lost. I was not going to fail HIM or the lost ones that must be found and brought back to live in the Word of Truth.

I know that many people can't make it to a church, and I get it that many people have physical ailments that restrict them to their homes. But that is no excuse for a capable Chosen Spiritual One to leave them in suffering without offering the inspiration for eternal life. I am a witness of my Lord Jesus Christ, who brought His love to me at the very young age of five and anointed me with His Holy Spirit. He showed me that He is the Church, and I started to believe in Him with all my heart, Spirit, and mind before I read a single verse in any bible. The Truth is in my Lord Jesus Christ. He is Lord over all creation, and since it was His will to have anointed me at a young age without the confusion of scholars, so be it; it is done. I am His servant forever, and His will has become my will. And since it is His will for me to help Him bring His Chosen Spiritual Ones to our GOD the Father, so be it; it is being done.

The Children of GOD have been lied to throughout the millennia. The Keys to the Kingdom of Heaven have been hidden from the Children of GOD far too long by the corruption of humanity. We all have the capability to receive the Spirit of our Lord Jesus Christ and the Holy Spirit of our GOD the Father to be One with us at anytime, anywhere, without a doubt or fear; by having the sincerity in the repenting of our sins and accepting our Lord Jesus Christ to help us keep His commands.

As a Chosen One, I do not ever fear because there is no fear in love. Do not fear GOD because HE loves you and wants you to love HIM and Worship HIM in Spirit with eternal life. You are HIS Child, and you please HIM by loving, accepting, and honoring HIS Son, Jesus Christ. Submit and commit yourself to our GOD the Father through HIS Son Jesus Christ to receive the Holy Spirit in complete unity as One with your Spirit. Continue to learn the teachings of our Lord Jesus Christ. Keep His commands and always love each other, to care for each other as much as He does care for you. This is the Key, and He is the Way to enter the Kingdom of Heaven.

For those who don't know the truth, do not understand the truth, and cannot stand to go to church just to leave without knowing the truth, I understand what you are going through. For those who do not have my Lord Jesus Christ, just believe this one thing: that you are considered one of the lost and my Lord Jesus Christ is trying to reach you through the Holy Spirit to give you eternal life.

Until you decide to clear your mind of all the distracting corruption of the world, then accept the help of my Lord Jesus Christ to realize that you are more valuable to Him and my GOD the Father than you can possibly imagine you are. Without accepting HIS Son, you will not have the Word of Truth to cross over from living in death to living eternal life in Spirit at this time while living in your Body-Temple. By remaining condemned, the non-believers of this world will see judgment, shame, and the final Second Death of their spirit for the cowering act of not standing in righteousness, and instead remaining in sin. You should know by now that it is no longer a secret who is responsible for your actions that will lead to your death or eternal life; it is by your own decision to live alone as you are, stand as you are, or decide to stand where you can: living in Spirit. This is the Word, and it is the Truth.

As a Chosen Spiritual One by the Chrism of the Child from my Lord Jesus Christ, the faith I have in my Lord Jesus Christ is directly proportional to my sanctification by the Word of Truth given to me through my Lord Jesus Christ for my salvation that He gave me with the power of His eternal life. I have received life eternal from Him by accepting the Complete Unity of His Spirit with and in my Spirit as One. As I live in their love, I have no fear and no sin that I was not forgiven, so that I may not see shame or judgment. Their Spirits are one with mine for life eternal, truth, forethought, foreknowledge, and the incorruptibility in them. I am created me in Spirit, and I am recreated me in Spirit complete unity to live Holy in Spirit with eternal life now in this Earthly Realm and later in the Eternal Spirit Realm. Regardless of how I received what I have, I must continuously practice living in the Spirit while keeping His commands for my own perfection living in the Spirit now without delay.

As one of the lost, you have not been told the truth, or you would have already understood it and lived by it now if you were willing to be a Holy in Spirit person. The hidden truth is that there are many who are lost and somehow are already keeping the commands naturally because their nature is already good. That may not be enough to find the path that leads to my Lord Jesus Christ for salvation. They may only need a little tune up by keeping the commands of committing to a decision to accept the gift of life by learning to live by the Testimony of GOD concerning HIS Son Jesus Christ. This must be one of the most hidden secrets of all time: in this day and age, no one will understand or experience the love of GOD without accepting our Lord Jesus Christ and the Holy Spirit of GOD the Father into their own Spirit to become One in Spirit with them first. This is not a catch twenty-two situation; it is a do-or-die twice situation; first, in flesh; then, in spirit, which is the final Second Death of a person if they do not accept Him.

The Word of Truth is revealed in the experience of living with the Word of Truth, who is alive in the Chosen Spiritual One. My Lord Jesus Christ is the living Word of Truth. Only then will you feel the life of them living in you, with you, for you, and for others. The better you get in tune with the Living Light of the Holy Spirit they put in you, the more blessings and goodness come to you and out of you. Only then will you become stronger and more faithful with the ability to help other Chosen Spiritual Ones stand in the truth to share in the love of our Lord Jesus Christ as our brothers and sisters. The Holy Spirit Family of Chosen Spiritual Ones are constantly growing as we suffer to rid ourselves of sin and live the Holy Life that we are called to live by our GOD the Father through our Lord Jesus Christ, as our own Spirit is guided to the truth by the Holy Spirit as One with us.

As Chosen Ones, we are constantly seeking for the lost. Whenever I find one, I enjoy revealing the truth to them the best I can. To me, it's like healing the sick, or teaching a baby that you love them and that you are with them to help them have no fear. We're on the same Spirit Family team, but the truth is that I cannot heal everyone: only the ones I am led to. In other words, I can reach only the ones who trust me, understand how I talk, and know that I am telling them the truth for their own good as well as mine because I am a Chosen Spiritual One who knows the way to the Word of Truth through my Lord Jesus Christ. They will only listen to me because we speak each other's language. They were brought to me by the Spirit, as I was led to them to know their Spirit. This is why it's so important that I learn to keep the truth the best that I can because someone I will know and care about needs to hear the truth to be saved now. I may be the only one in the world who will bring it for them to understand how to accept my Lord Jesus Christ before they die in sin to remain condemned, then die the Second Death of their Spirit in the place where Death itself will also be destroyed forever in the Lake of Fire of burning sulfur. That is the place where the spirit of non-believers will be destroyed forever. So, if Death is non-existent by the power in the Fire, then the Condemned will also be non-existent as my GOD the Father will have removed all the condemned sinners, so we may live in Spirit Perfection in the Spirit Realm without a thought of sin or Death.

This is how important it is for us to learn the truth and accept it as soon as we can: if one person doesn't get saved, one or more people or their children may not be saved through them because someone didn't have the courage to help them. We must have the courage to have eternal life within ourselves so we may help others and their children. For those who become cowards and remain in sin, it is a shame anyway you look at it. If we have any sense of decency in our lives to become good people, we should, without hesitation, step up and help people bring their babies up to know our Lord Jesus Christ for eternal life. The religion of caring for widows and orphans is the same as keeping oneself in the will of my GOD the Father through my Lord Jesus Christ. And it is the only acceptable religion by HIM.

This is an example of how simple it is to do it. Our Lord Jesus Christ went to the poor, sick, and uneducated people who had nothing, and at that time may have only known how to farm for a living. They may not have known how to read or write. Only by speaking to them were some of them able to understand the Truth in the Word. The truth is simple and is a very light burden on people. It's easy to enjoy living in the Spirit. Just keep His commands and become efficient at helping others do the same. Then our Lord Jesus Christ will bless you and them with eternal life now and later for seeking the lost and turning them to Him for eternal salvation.

All I wish to do, as I seek the lost, is introduce my Lord Jesus Christ to those people who are being called to know Him and my GOD the Father, so they may receive eternal salvation by the gift of HIS Eternal Life that HE has put in HIS Son, my Lord Jesus Christ. Seeking the lost and returning them to my GOD the Father is HIS will, the will of my Lord Jesus Christ, and my will as I live in Spirit.

Chapter 16 - Little Miracles

I continued to pray in the Spirit every day without fail while I wrote what I was inspired to write through the Holy Spirit. When I wasn't writing, I would minister the Word of Truth to anyone who asked for help to learn. Whenever I could find someone to listen and learn the truth, I was compelled to share with them what I had written. Along the way, I would be shown a sign that the power through my Lord Jesus Christ was still with me and working in me with the Holy Spirit of my GOD the Father. I was eager to share with others how He shows Himself to me in Spirit through the little miracles that I recognize are miraculous signs from Him, while others might brush them off as coincidences. But, as a Chosen Spiritual One, I am not able to ignore the signs that are gifted to me any longer. I have been transformed in Spirit prayer to constantly be searching on autopilot by the will to hear everything the Holy Spirit was leading me to understand in the Word of Truth. I am always ready to listen through Him because I know what He tells me is what my Lord Jesus Christ wants me to know, do, and say for the purpose of worshipping my GOD the Father.

My mindset has become more and more like my Lord Jesus Christ by believing that no one who needs Him gets turned away from Him, as everyone who is condemned by sin is worthy of hearing and accepting the truth to become sanctified for salvation from our own condemnation that we must reject for living in the Spirit of Truth. Therefore, I would minister the truth in the word and counsel with the Chosen Spiritual Ones who were imprisoned and developing a powerful movement of ministry for our Lord Jesus Christ. The ministry was transitioning to the outside of the prison gates by the perseverance of the Chosen Spiritual Ones who were forging a path to freedom by spreading the Gospel of my Lord Jesus Christ, who brings the power of His Spirit into anyone who so loves Him to have His mercy within them.

Three disciples in the Word of Truth, who in particular go by the names Emmanuel, Donnie, and George, would trade scriptures, share testimony, and help the authors within the gates develop literature for self-improvement programs. They may not realize that their faith against the adversity they had to overcome in their own personal lives gave me a higher level of inspiration to continue on my appointed mission, living in Spirit. I have no excuse if they don't have any excuse for living by the commands of my Lord Jesus Christ. The actions of our character speak for themselves as we live in control of ourselves by the power of our Spirit living in Complete Unity. Nothing is impossible with GOD to bring HIS commands to the world, even through a man, woman, or child who has nothing to give but themself and will do so as a Child of GOD committed to HIS Word of Truth through our Lord Jesus Christ.

I remember that Donnie had asked me to keep in touch with him if I could help Him on His journey to get closer to the Lord. I agreed because I am a Chosen Spiritual One commanded to minister for my Lord Jesus Christ to all His children who are being called to our GOD the Father, no matter who or where they are in the world. Little did we know, the Holy Spirit of GOD the Father was already actively spearheading the merging of the missions we were on, and that by our faith, we remained together with Him.

After retiring, it didn't seem to me like I had much more to say to Donnie for his salvation until the Holy Spirit compelled me to write a letter to Him in Spirit prayer. My Lord Jesus Christ confirmed it with another little miracle that just blew my mind and enlightened my Spirit to an amazing level of understanding. I couldn't remember the Holy Spirit working within me that strongly before, so I knew that I was being led in a new direction that would be revealed to me very soon. It's impossible for me not to believe that my Lord Jesus Christ and the Holy Spirit from my GOD the Father are within me. They make my heart jump with love and joy of understanding when I least expect it. That's when I turn to HIM and praise HIM stronger in Spirit prayer every day in the Name of HIS Son Jesus Christ. It's truly a good feeling to just let it all flow from my heart at those times. Don't ever hold back the love you feel for our GOD the Father through our Lord Jesus Christ.

VINCENTE GARCIA

Because loving GOD with all our heart, mind, and Spirit is what we are recreated to do naturally in Spirit.

I started the letter to Donnie with the usual courtesies and got stuck on two paragraphs. Of course, I had to pray in Spirit for the right way to say what I needed to tell him. It was difficult to get the words out because this letter had to be perfectly written for his inspiration to remain on the path of his mission, and for him to contemplate every blessing he has ever received from our Lord Jesus Christ, which is essential for everyone who is living as a Chosen Spiritual One on their Spiritual path.

I finally managed to write the letter, and decided to print it and read it to myself out loud to make sure what I was compelled to write made sense to me. The page printed out perfectly, as I had typed it, but before I could take the letter out of the printer tray, something else started to print. I thought to myself, I know I didn't write more than a page; this shouldn't be printing something else. I picked up both pages and looked at the letter I had written, which came out perfect. When I looked at the other page that was printed, I recognized that it had one of the paragraphs that I was struggling with printed at the top of the page, and that the other paragraph that I had struggled with was printed on the bottom of the other side of the page. So, I turned the page right side up, and I started to read what it said. Then I began to realize that this was a little miracle message from my Lord Jesus Christ for all the Chosen Spiritual Ones. It stated that I must tell all His Children who I know that it is important for every one of them to write down their own testimonials: firstly, to help us remember them and never forget all the things that He has done for each one of us throughout our lives, and secondly, to share those little miracles with each other as necessary to help inspire each other. We all must know that it is our Lord Jesus Christ who is living in us as One family and in One Spirit as Holy Children of our GOD the Father.

By the time I had finished both paragraphs, I had tears running down my face in amazement that my Lord Jesus Christ had once again reached out to me and opened my heart to receive a message from Him by using the printer to give me the message and confirm it, so I would know that it was also meant for me to know and do. This message was not random; it was a deliberate spoken language given to me in a way that triggered in my heart for me to become enlightened with the power of the Holy Spirit to make me know the Truth in the Word and to experience it in a whole new, different language, which is another way of speaking to me.

In other words, it meant a lot of different things to me at the same time in this Earthly Realm and the Spirit Realm. I felt like I was acknowledged by them for the things I have done. That is my enlightenment from knowledge by understanding what had taken place, especially for me to experience it by all means, and that I am following the will of my GOD the Father in Spirit prayer.

At the times I receive a little miracle, I am once again renewed to know that I am indisputably a Child of my GOD the Father who received the Chrism by HIS Son and my Lord Jesus Christ, and I am being guided by HIS Holy Spirit as One with them in Complete Unity. I'm not usually emotional, but when these little miracles happen, sometimes I can't turn off my tear faucets. They're the tears of joy, happiness, and the love for humanity with a complete fulfillment by the power of the Holy Spirit within me; that must be how our Lord Jesus Christ feels for each one of us who accepts Him by knowing the potential of the eternal life that He has waiting for us to decide to accept and start living alive in the Spirit with Him. He sees us go from death to eternal life with Him; that is, being recreated a second time, which some people know as being reborn, which actually means being recreated in Spirit as One in Complete Unity with them in the Holy of Holiest place in our Body-Temple, the Bridal Chamber, and our most central place within us.

Some people may have been confused to think they should feel unworthy of our Lord Jesus Christ because of the sin that they had once committed, but the truth is on the contrary. We are worthy of forgiveness for our sincere repenting of our sins to our GOD the Father in the Name of HIS Son Jesus Christ. Anyone who does not believe this is living sinisterly and condemned in their conditional lie that leads to death. Not believing that you are worthy of eternal life is the same as rejecting the Testimony of our GOD the Father and the purpose of having our Lord Jesus Christ for us to live a holy life now in Complete Unity. To accept my Lord Jesus Christ, I must always believe one hundred percent, without a doubt or any fear, as I follow His commands because I have Him with me and I love Him.

As a Chosen Spiritual One, there is no doubt in my mind for me to know that no one gets to feel that blessed, that loved, and that close to GOD if they are unworthy. The truth is, the reason why I feel worthy is because of my Lord Jesus Christ having the power to forgive me of my sin; through the Holy Spirit, He enlightens me in every way. He makes the time especially for me, specifically to make a special way for me to understand what He is showing me so that I know that I am completely worthy of His love, and the love of my GOD the Father, or He wouldn't take the time to show me anything in the diverse ways that He does if He didn't love me.

Showing Himself to His believers is exactly what He said that He would do for everyone who believes in Him and follows His commands, because that shows that we love Him and He acknowledges us in that way. And that's why sometimes I cry for His love when I see the power of His truth through every little miracle He does to show me that He is always with me, like He said He would be. I take every little miracle and line them all up in chronological order to compare the differences of each one to notice that He never ceases to amaze me with the possibilities of how He can get His messages through to me, penetrating my very existence that supports me on my Spiritual path for Spiritual perfection. I can't help but feel so grateful every time it happens because I know that as weak as I am, He loves me. I know that He will never let me down so long as I continue to follow Him and keep His commands.

I see everything that He has gifted specifically for me, so I may know that He is recreating me to become who I am supposed to be in Spirit. I vow to live up to those gifts that He has recreated me worthy of; without His love in me, I would be nothing, hollow, and worthless. This is the Word, and it is the Truth. Now I am compelled to share my testimony with others to help them understand what is the true inspiration from our GOD the Father through HIS Son Jesus Christ and HIS Holy Spirit becoming One with our Spirit.

Another little miracle happened when I was finishing the book, Inspiration for Your Eternal Life. I was using my computer in the read-aloud playback mode to listen to what I had typed. It was speaking the words of a scripture where a rich man had fallen to his knees in front of Jesus Christ and asked Him what the greatest commandment in the Law was. At the same time, I was praying in Spirit with a question held in my mind. I asked, "Lord, what is the main message in this book that I am writing for His people?" At that very moment, the playback voice went off script from reading the typed words and said, "Always Love Each Other." Those words were the answer to the question that was in my mind, which was not printed on that page. Then, without skipping a beat, it continued back to the script to read the next line that it was supposed to read aloud, which is the greatest commandment: to love the LORD your GOD with all your heart, soul, and mind.

I stopped the playback and said, "Please let me record this with my phone so I can bring inspiration to all the ones I have been texting the daily Word to and so I can have proof to bring glory to my GOD the Father." I grabbed my phone and started recording it, and it did it again. I was able to send the video out to everyone as proof that GOD works in every conceivable way to reach us, and that nothing is impossible for HIM. People were texting me back while saying that they had chills running over them and praising the power of my Lord Jesus Christ. There is no limitation to how the Holy Spirit will speak to you and lead you to the truth. Once again, I was given tangible proof that my Lord Jesus Christ is with me in Spirit.

VINCENTE GARCIA

This next little miracle was a test of the heart for me to be a witness to, and it proved that my wife was becoming closer to the power of our GOD the Father. This is how she learned to know that she should never doubt her true feelings and emotions, no matter how little they affected her. Even more importantly, she learned to never say or do anything without first giving thanks to our GOD the Father in Spirit prayer, and in the Name of HIS Son our Lord Jesus Christ, to establish our steps in everything that we should say or do and only if it is HIS will for us.

On a late afternoon, she had received a phone call from a close relative inviting us to go to dinner that night in another state two hours away. Without hesitation in her excitement, she agreed to go. A few minutes later after hanging up, she told me that she had made these plans for us. I wasn't pushing the issue when I asked her if she had already agreed to go because I was feeling hesitant to tell her that I was feeling and thinking it wasn't a good idea to go. The thought in my mind was that it was so far away and that it was too late in the day to go there, but either way I felt resistance. There could be an accident on the road, or something could delay us. I didn't have a good feeling about the way she was responding to me questioning the idea of traveling that night, and I began to think that this plan was not going to turn out well. At the same time I thought that I may have overreacted, so I agreed to go and see how it would turn out.

LITTLE MIRACLES

While she was getting ready, she said she felt bothered about agreeing to go without asking me first, so I asked her to just call back and cancel before it got too late. Her response was that she would go alone if I wanted to stay home. Of course, I said, "No way. I want to see how this is going to turn out." I wasn't going to let her travel so far away alone, anyway. As we got in the car and started on our way, she began to get emotional and tear up about how bad she felt for not asking me before she agreed to go. That was her feelings in her heart letting her know that something wasn't right. I think she wanted to cancel, but she also was frustrated because she didn't want to disappoint the ones who invited us. I reassured her that I wasn't upset; I was concerned and I wanted to drive her there because I saw that she was nervous and in no condition to be driving with tears flowing down her face. I helped her relax, and told her that we would be careful and just take our time as we went. We could find out together how the Lord was going to make the trip turn out.

After driving for about half an hour, we crossed into the next state and noticed there was a roadblock across all lanes of the highway in both directions with a Highway Patrol Officer diverting cars away from the road to take a side road detour. We knew that this was not a good thing and that we needed to find out what the problem was on the highway since we only had one other alternate road to take that was five miles away. Of course, the alternate road was blocked too. After inquiring for a solution, we found out there was a car racing event that was going to keep the roads closed for the next three days. That's when I saw the sigh of relief in her demeanor, and we both thanked GOD through our Lord Jesus Christ for revealing the truth to us together. That was the time that we knew we were being taught that we must trust our feelings for each other, and that we were being given the way to follow the guidance of HIS Holy Spirit to the Truth as our Lord Jesus Christ showed us through this situation.

We agreed to remember to never do anything in Word or Deed without asking the Holy Spirit of our GOD the Father to guide us by HIS will, first by giving thanks to HIM in the Name of HIS Son, Jesus Christ. My Lord Jesus Christ was telling us not to go all along. He has His reasons, and they are to keep us safe on our Spiritual path. We must always remember to pay attention to the "Little Miracles" that we are given to bless us on our Spiritual path as Chosen Spiritual Ones being led by the Holy Spirit in faith, power, patience, and self-control. Without a doubt or any fear, we learn to trust in the little miracles of our GOD the Father to keep us on HIS path for our salvation through our Lord Jesus Christ and HIS Holy Spirit within us.

Chapter 17 - Foreknowledge

All things in the truth will be revealed to me through my Lord Jesus Christ. By this wisdom as a Chosen One, I learn how to ask for the things that I need to glorify my GOD the Father. I don't ask to elevate myself; I ask to humble myself as I become who HE wants me to become by HIS will, and HE will elevate me by HIS will at the appropriate time through HIS Son and HIS Holy Spirit, who guides me to do and say HIS will.

I give thanks in Spirit prayer without any fear or doubt to my GOD the Father for the things that HE will give me through the Name of HIS Son, my Lord Jesus Christ, because that is how a Chosen One must ask of HIM. The Holy Spirit that comes out from my GOD the Father and into my heart tells HIM what I need before I know that I need to ask.

Now I can see myself as a fourth one with them in the Kingdom of Heaven, as the Holy Spirit tells me and shows me what is to come, and that is Him telling me my future. In the Kingdom of Heaven within me, there is my GOD the Father as One with my Lord Jesus Christ and the Holy Spirit, all in complete unity as One with my Spirit and all within my Body-Temple. When my Body-Temple dies in this Earthly Realm, my Spirit will be raised up to live in the Spirit Realm with them in the Heavenly Realm of perfection.

VINCENTE GARCIA

As a Child of Light, I truly know who I am as a Chosen Spiritual One, where I came from, and to where I will return. I am thoroughly aware that my GOD the Father longs for HIS Holy Spirit that HE put in me to become one with my Spirit, therefore HE longs for me as well and more than I can possibly know. This is why I contemplate on things in heaven as I was taught by my Lord Jesus Christ, and this is why I constantly strive to help refine my own actions, character, and nature to live up to the Resurrection that I have been given the Chrism to live as a Holy Child of GOD in everything I do and say on earth as it is in heaven.

That is the foreknowledge that I have become blessed with, as in being anointed with in Spirit, by having been given the Chrism with the Holy Spirit as an advocate within me, helping me become stronger in faith for the glory of my GOD the Father. So, I have to describe this, as I have been blessed with a higher grace with the power of my GOD the Father flowing through me at all times. That is living in the Spirit without doubt or fear as I wait patiently for the next foreknowledge in a vision, sign, symbol, dream, sound, vibration, or whisper so I will know what to do to overcome the temptations of this realm and do the will of my GOD the Father. We must all learn to live this way. I stopped making my own choices by giving myself up to HIM completely in Spirit prayer and began living in Spirit by the will of my GOD the Father.

FOREKNOWLEDGE

When praying in Spirit, it became easier for me as I continued to learn with the help of the Holy Spirit with me. The Holy Spirit is infinitely Superior to our limited minds. I wished to be shown certain things to know the answers that will give me clarity in my mind. So, I ask for wisdom in order to be taught how foreknowledge works in my life now. I have been aware that it was happening to me, but I wanted to test my ability to recognize it in the Word of Truth and act accordingly when it did. I feel the need to practice living with the Holy Spirit now, while I have time to learn at my own pace and sharpen my skills interacting with Him.

I was finding out that foreknowledge works in several ways as soon as I was ready to receive it in good faith. Without being ready in faith without doubt, as if what I ask for has already been given, I cannot receive anything from my GOD the Father through my Lord Jesus Christ. I must believe without a doubt in my heart, mind, and in Spirit that my GOD the Father will give me anything I need to glorify HIM. Blessings are something that cannot be controlled or forced; they are given to me as a gift to receive, and it is to be received as gracefully as possible, as I am living by faith in the Spirit, with the Holy Spirit showing me the skills I was blessed with because of my faith. Belief without fear or doubt is the strength of my faith.

Time is not a limiting factor as to how or when I receive foreknowledge. I can receive a message in one day and see the results of the answer that fulfills it within the same day, or it could happen as a surprise to test my ability to recognize it quickly, or it could be answered 50 years later, depending on how much interaction I need, which is required for me to learn why it was delivered to me. Whatever the way it's delivered to me or the reason for it, I must always embrace the power of patience with a love for truth, which is embracing the power of my GOD the FATHER, HIS Son Jesus Christ, and HIS Holy Spirit as One with my Spirit in Complete Unity.

Whatever the circumstances are in my life as a Chosen Spiritual One, it is always to my benefit to keep up with HIS Holy Spirit while maintaining my patience and readiness to act. I cannot say I'm ready; He knows and tells me when I'm ready after I have been conditioned by Him for the task. It's a refining process of my faith and will to find out what He wants me to learn, so I can keep it in my heart forever to have that wisdom as my Spiritual growth. Whatever way I am given a message, it gets burned into my memory to be recalled at the exact time I need to remember it without trying, like it had happened a minute earlier. At that time, I will have a prophecy to live up to that becomes my past as I learned to live up to it in my present for my fulfilling of it in my future event. I must constantly live to master my present for living my future in the Spirit realm.

FOREKNOWLEDGE

These messages are given to me to contemplate in Spirit prayer whenever I can, and for me to ask my questions so I will be prepared to act as necessary in accordance with the Word of Truth to save my life and sometimes the lives of others. They may also be given to me to help me turn a dangerous situation into a safe one and to help me live a blessed life in peace and harmony with others. As I live my life in Spirit through my Lord Jesus Christ while being guided by the Holy Spirit, my life has become a reflection of what I contemplate in the Heavenly Realm as I keep my mind compelled to glorify my GOD the Father.

During that summer, I spent a lot of time in my swimming pool. I would block out all the problems of the world from my mind. Then I would focus on my GOD the Father and give thanks to HIM through my Lord Jesus Christ for everything HE has blessed me with. I always acknowledge my Lord Jesus Christ when I praise and give thanks to my GOD the Father, as my Lord Jesus Christ has taught me to.

Then there was a day when a question came to my mind that I asked in all seriousness: "What do you want me to become?" After the thought of that question cleared from my mind, I kept it hidden in my memory and waited for the answer as I stared intently into the water and then looked into my mind to see if an answer would appear. Suddenly, while keeping my mind clear of distractions and without thoughts except knowing that

VINCENTE GARCIA

I was waiting for an answer, the word PERFECT appeared like I was looking right at it with both eyes, crystal clear in my mind. It will remain there for me to remember for the rest of my life. I asked in Spirit prayer without any fear or doubt, waited patiently, and received the answer. The answer is that my GOD the Father wants me to become perfect like my Lord Jesus Christ is perfect, and that HE is telling me how much HE loves me. HE loves me like HIS Son Jesus Christ in me; He loves me like HIS Holy Spirit in me; HE loves me like the Spirit I am recreated to become perfect.

The very next thing I thought was, "This is why I must remain attached to my Lord Jesus Christ. Because without Him, I am nothing now and will become nothing later. The truth is, only by having Him with me as One am I given the Spirit of His perfection to fulfill me to the level of His perfection to become a Holy Child of Light for my GOD the Father. I literally feel like I have become the whole person that I am recreated me to become, maturely living in the Spirit for a little while in this Earthly Realm as I become ready to be transformed into a higher grace at the time of my redemption by the transformation into a Spirit-Body in the eternal Spirit Realm.

Now I have the foreknowledge of what I will become in my future with my Lord Jesus Christ. I will be perfect in the presence of my GOD in HIS New Kingdom on HIS New Earth, conjoined with a New Heaven that HE will make perfect for my home with HIM. That is HIS will, the will of HIS Son, my Lord Jesus Christ, and now it's my will to become perfect for my GOD the Father.

Once again, my prayer was answered that summer as I found myself in my garage swatting at moths that had found a way to get into my garage every day. I got good at catching them – except for one. That one would fly and hide as soon as I walked anywhere near it. I chased it for a couple of days and couldn't get it. It was the smartest and most elusive moth in the world, and it was a vicious challenge that was testing me to catch it. It was a challenge I was not willing to lose. Whenever I couldn't find it, I would wait for another time to try again.

Later on, one night as I was in prayer authoring my book, I felt a strong presence in Spirit. I asked the Holy Spirit to show me a vision of something that would happen soon to test my ability to recognize the vision when it happened, so I may act accordingly in Spirit. Some people might call this kind of experience Déjà vu, and scientists can't explain what it is or why ninety-seven percent of people have experienced it, or why it is more common in young people.

As a Chosen Spiritual One, I must follow the guidance of my Lord Jesus Christ through the Holy Spirit. Living in the Spirit Realm is how I can better understand the Truth in the Word and learn to know the language of the

VINCENTE GARCIA

Holy Spirit, which is superior to the limitations of science. This is how I know my Lord Jesus Christ is speaking to me: He uses my memory for the things that He has shown me to remember, so I may learn to interpret what is being said first for a later time. Because it is made uniquely for me to learn pertaining to the Spiritual path that I must walk in my life. Ninety-seven percent of people can testify that these kinds of memory recalls happen without knowing why. Now you know why and how it happens.

So, the Holy Spirit showed me a vision in my mind of a moth standing right in front of me on my garage floor, as clear as if it were happening just then, as realistically as if I were actually living in the vision in my mind, focusing on a moth standing on the floor. He let me know that as soon as this vision happened, I would have enough time to step on it or swat it to have no more moths in my garage. So, I thought, "The next time I get a chance to look for that moth, I'm going to check the floor, and when I see the moth on the floor, I'm going to have time to end the challenge."

The next morning, there was only one moth in the garage, and it wasn't on the floor. It was business as usual; it was evading me any time I walked toward it. Then, after a couple of minutes of chasing it, something different happened; it flew straight at my face, and I had to move so it wouldn't hit my eye. I felt the edges of its wings fluttering on my face before it flew away from me.

FOREKNOWLEDGE

Then it turned back around toward me and flew really hard into the side of my ribs before it landed and was standing on the floor directly in front of me.

And there it was: the vision I had been expecting to see come true. This so-called "Déjà vu" happened just as I remembered it at that very moment from the time it had been hidden in the memory of my mind. My thought of the vision in the past was my foreknowledge of my future, and the vision I was living in my present all became one thought in its entirety as it manifested from my memory into the present Earthly Realm to become the past the moment I saw it and was living through it. It was exactly the vision hidden in my mind as I saw the moth on the floor the day before. From that moment on, it was no longer foreknowledge; it was simply a past experience that I had taken with me into the future to become enlightened by Spirit knowledge. I fulfilled the prophecy at the time my past, present, and future came together. So I experienced living my future, during my present, and it all became my past.

Living in Spirit, I am mastering my present to live up to my future that will become my past. This is the superior Spiritual language by foreknowledge from the Holy Spirit, which is to this day misunderstood by scientists, and is commonly known in the world as "Déjà vu" for those who forget and have no explanation or understanding for what has happened to themselves. This is how the Holy Spirit has always been reaching out to me throughout my lifetime. And now I know it is what He does to reach out to others to become aware of their own Spiritual side of their own creation as a way of calling them to find out how and why they are created this way. The question that remains is: are you fearless enough to find out the truth? The truth is, we are created to acknowledge and worship our Living GOD the Father, through HIS Son.

As I looked down at the moth, it stayed perfectly still, like it was standing up tall to give me the chance to do what was on my mind. All I had to do was step on it or swat it, and the challenge would be over, but at that exact time I could hear the Holy Spirit ask, "Are you going to step on it?" When I checked myself for the answer, I answered, "No. I can't hurt this one, and I want it to live because it tried so hard to live that I don't feel like it deserves to die." I looked at the moth standing in front of me, perfectly still for a few more seconds, then it looked like it became unfrozen as it moved its wings up and down a couple of times before I watched it fly up onto the wall near the garage door. I opened the garage door and let it fly out. After contemplating everything I had done, I felt good about how I handled that experience in its entirety. I felt a connection to everything at the same time, even the little moth who kissed my face with a soft flutter of its wings. In that lesson, I learned that we must let the Spirit flow through us. We are not trying to control our Spirit; we are learning to set it free. Free from the

FOREKNOWLEDGE

insanity of being trapped in this Realm on Earth in the flesh. After living in Complete Unity and maturing in Spirit through these types of interactions with my Lord Jesus Christ through the Holy Spirit, I will always believe in Him without any fear or doubt. Those two words don't manifest as truth any longer in a Chosen Spiritual One who has learned the Word of Truth.

The Holy Spirit gives me the time I need to react to a vision, whether by infusing my mind with the knowledge that I may need to have at a higher rate of learning, which may appear to be as if time has stopped or slowed down to give me the opportunity to experience the entire vision in detail as it is actively recording into my memory. The question that remains is how I act after receiving this gift of foreknowledge. Firstly, I must recognize that what I am being shown is for my Spiritual growth. Secondly, my action will reveal my Spiritual character at the time I experience it in my future, which displays the maturity of my Spiritual growth in comparison to the Word of GOD in which I have practiced living by the commands HE has given to learn through HIS Son, Jesus Christ, my Lord, Savior, Church, and Teacher. I thank my GOD the Father in the Name of HIS Son Jesus Christ for sending me HIS Holy Spirit to guide me with foreknowledge to stand in the Word of Truth.

My Spirit is constantly being refined through my thoughts and actions in everything I do and say to glorify my GOD the Father through my Lord Jesus Christ by following the guidance of the Holy Spirit in Complete Unity within my Body-Temple. This is the way I am guided to mature in Spirit Holiness from purification by the sanctification of my mind, body, and Spirit, which leads to perfection and holiness inside and out. This is how the Holy Spirit leads me as a Chosen Spiritual One to stay attached to my Lord Jesus Christ for His gift of salvation for me to live in Spirit now with the eternal life that only He has the authority to give to all the people who believe in Him and follow His commands.

Within the next week, we had some family guests over for a weekend in the pool for the first time. It was a wonderful time for us because we seldom got to see them. We wanted everything to be a perfect time together as we aimed to treat them to a memorable staycation with us since they rarely took time off from work together to travel or visit. After a relaxing time in the pool, enjoying the summer sunrays, we all settled into the living room to catch up on old times.

Then, I remembered the day before that I saw my wife stocking the wine cooler with her favorites. So, I asked the ladies if they would like to share a bottle of red wine as they relaxed on the sofas, and of course, they said, "Yes." Without hesitation, I walked over to the wine cooler, which was positioned behind the bar and under the countertop between two built-in cabinets. As I opened the wine cooler door, I saw that the top shelf

FOREKNOWLEDGE

was over stacked and that bottles had started sliding out, so I quickly placed my left forearm across the bottles to push them back up in place, as I quickly braced myself by holding on to the top of the bar on my right and I held myself still in that position to get my bearings. I was thinking this would not be a good day if the bottles were to fall out and break on the tile floor, which would ruin our perfect weekend having to clean up glass and red wine out of the tile grout.

I was looking down at my bare feet on the tile as I was holding the bottles back in the wine cooler with my left forearm, when the unthinkable happened. I saw a bottle of wine slide out over my left forearm, and in a very slow motion I watched it drop straight down and hit flat on its side onto the tile floor, then the bottle cracked open, spreading glass and wine all over the tile and onto my bare foot. I was instantly surprised to become aware that the foreknowledge I just saw was my immediate future, and the wine bottle had just flipped over my arm and was still in mid-air as it was just starting to drop straight down toward the tile and I knew exactly where it was going to hit the tile squarely, since I just saw it already happen in slow motion.

Then, in a split second, I felt the power of the Holy Spirit jolt through me as He took control of me and quickly helped me shift my weight to my right foot to kick my left foot forward and turn it to the right a little, just enough to catch the bottle of wine in mid-air with the top of my foot before it struck the tile. If I tried to think this all out, it would have been too late. I slowly reached down with my right hand and took the bottle off my left foot where it was balanced across the top of my toes, and I carefully placed the bottle on the bottom shelf. Then, I properly rearranged the wine cooler before I served two beautiful and happy ladies their red wine for a wonderful visit.

I realized that experience was a test of how in tune I was with the Holy Spirit and that I must remember how fast the Holy Spirit can show me a vision, answer it, and help me take action. The Holy Spirit also taught me that He can take control of my body to physically help me when I am in need of His help. When my Lord Jesus Christ says the Holy Spirit will be with me, He means as One with me. As I have learned time and time again, I just have to believe it and do what must be done without any fear or doubt. Nevertheless, the weekend turned out to be like the good times we had always wished to have with our friends and family.

My lessons did not stop there. As I was immersed in writing my first book, Inspiration For Your Eternal Life, I would pose the question in my mind to the Holy Spirit from time to time about when the writing of this book would be completed. The answer was, "You will not stop writing until after the editor is chosen." It wasn't too much longer before the answer would come to me as a vision-dream to be revealed to me at a later time.

FOREKNOWLEDGE

This vision-dream had many signs and symbols to confirm that only I would understand, as it pertained to how I was becoming enlightened throughout my life, so that there would be no mistake to know who and when the Chosen Spiritual Editor would be revealed to me. This is what I have learned to understand what revelations mean. I must live through revelations throughout my life as I am led to them for Spiritual Knowledge. Everyone should know it's the truth as my Lord Jesus Christ has taught me, and that the Holy Spirit will lead me to the truth in what is to come to me later in my life.

As a Chosen One, first I am given a message that my Spirit prayer has been heard when it is, and second, I am later given evidence when the Spirit prayer has been answered. This is why it is so important to remember to keep up with the guidance of the Holy Spirit so we don't disrespectfully pray repeatedly over the prayers that we should already know have been heard and are being answered. When a Chosen One prays in Spirit without doubt to our GOD the Father in Spirit through our Lord Jesus Christ, to glorify our GOD the Father according to HIS will, the Chosen One believes what is prayed for has already been received.

In this next vision-dream that I was given, the first thing I did was I open my eyes and found myself in a void that surrounded me in pitch darkness, where nothing existed except at a distance. There was a room suspended by nothing that was lit up inside with a double door entryway without doors attached. I knew at that time that I was a Spirit of Light, but I did not see that I had a body form. I knew how to move with my mind through the void of darkness by focusing my mind to move toward the room, and I entered through the doorway into the large room and appeared there with my body that couldn't move like I did in Spirit. The room had a high ceiling with large double-pane windows on the walls on my left and my right, and there wasn't another doorway. It was filled with people who appeared poor and humble, with very little knowledge of the truth. They were hoping for someone to help them understand how to be set free from the captivity of that room, which seemed to be a realm that they did not know how to escape from. They were all very quiet about their situation, and by the look in their eyes, they were so poor in Spirit. They were all observing what I was going to do or say to see if I could help them in any way. I started to think that I was searching for something that could help us all, so I let them know that I would never stop searching for the truth, and I vowed that as soon as I could find a way to reveal the truth to them, I would return to them to help them learn how to become free from captivity.

Although I was still learning where I was, I listened to the Holy Spirit that was speaking in me and guiding me as I searched for the sign of the truth that I was compelled to find and I had no idea how it was going to be revealed to me when I found it. He told me that I couldn't stay there with them, and I could not go backwards from any way that I entered a room. I had to find a way out and I could only move forward as I continued to search for something that He would reveal to me when I had found it.

Since there were no other doorways, I looked out of the large double-pane windows that were as large as the double glass doors of a store. That's when I noticed that I was in an old building about five floors up that had a ledge just wide enough for me to stand on and side step along. So, I decided to walk on the ledge and see if I could find an open window to enter another room and exit through the door in that room. As I was moving with my back against the wall, sidestepping along the ledge, I looked down and thought, "If I misstep off this path just once, I could fall to my death." My body wanted to get off the ledge, and my Spirit was telling me to stay focused. The ledge is my path, and I shouldn't attempt to walk off of this path. It would be the end of me, and I couldn't let that happen because of my vow to help free the people and their children from the captivity of that room. I was aware of everything that was happening, and at the same time, I realized they didn't know where they were, and that was why they were depending on someone like me to help them in hopes of finding a better way of life for themselves.

VINCENTE GARCIA

As I continued to sidestep along the ledge of the building, I passed a few locked windows and looked inside many others just to find out they were empty or without anything I was searching for anyway. After passing a few more windows, I noticed a tall young man who appeared to be patiently waiting as he was looking out of one of the windows. He was a Holy and Spiritual man who was living in Spirit prayer as he waited, and I could tell he was expecting me. When he saw me, he opened one side of the window and reached out his hand to help pull me into the room. He didn't need to say a word because he knew why I was there. He respectfully took a few steps back and then stepped to my right side, revealing someone who was also waiting patiently and was there for me to meet.

There I saw a beautiful woman sitting in a chair in the middle of the room, facing me as I stood at the window. Between us and off to my left side and on her right was a table with glasses of water on it, and she pointed her hand with an open palm to the water and said, "Drink some water." I knew that everything I did in this room had a purpose, and that I had to pay close attention to everything that was happening because this room felt like a place of Holy Ceremony, and the ceremony was taking place. So, with all due respect, I accepted her offer with a courteous thank you and a slight bow of my head. I stepped up to the table with the water and carefully drank without spilling a drop. As I was drinking the water, I felt like I was drinking Water of Life that

FOREKNOWLEDGE

brought clarity and life to the words within me, and it was for the purpose of bringing forth a message that was to be written in a book to become a blessing to those who would read it to find the Word of Truth.

That is when the Holy Spirit let me know that she was the Chosen Spiritual One to be the Editor of all the things that He had been telling me about to write in prayer for over a year. I was to hand everything I wrote over to her in order to complete the manifestation of what my Lord Jesus Christ had compelled me to write through the Holy Spirit for the book to become properly manifested for people of the world to understand how to become inspired with Holy Spirit for eternal life.

As I continued to author the book, the memory of this vision was keeping me on track to write what I was led to explain as accurate to the format that I was told to. I knew that I had to reveal the Word and the Truth in it as perfectly as possible to help draw out the message and the purpose of what this book was being brought forth for in the world. I was being led to project a foundation for understanding the Truth in the Word of GOD for anyone who would be seeking to strengthen their faith every day to become inspired for salvation or remain attached to our Lord Jesus Christ to glorify our GOD the Father. By HIS will, we can now be glorified in the way HE provided for us to live in HIS New Covenant through HIS Son Jesus Christ for eternal life.

Knowing how foreknowledge works for a Chosen Spiritual One is directly proportional to understanding how we are expected to learn to live by the New Covenant of the Spirit, and how the Spirit language is explained for our understanding in this Earthly Realm of matter. Vision-dreams are but one language that helps us do just that, which means we are all learning new languages of the Spirit as we evolve in the understanding of ourselves and how we are being spoken to by our Lord Jesus Christ while living in Spirit. We must pay attention to the Holy Spirit to understand our unique purpose in this day and age, as we learn the purpose of living in all the Realms that we will stand in.

First, we must understand that the logic that we learn to hold onto for understanding the ways in this Earthly Realm of matter that is limited to basic language, rooted in its basic theories, and is only a reflection of the Superior Spirit Realm. Scientific Logic is of little value by its use of induction and deduction for explaining the ability to evolve spiritually. Living by the Spirit is the superior form of intelligence that speaks in multiple dimensions at the same time that can only be experienced by the Chosen Spiritual One who believes without doubt or fear and is effectively interacting and living by the Spirit in Complete Unity.

Chosen Ones are gifted with abilities that transcend the limited scientific logic of the mortal person to become reborn and spiritually transformed by the

FOREKNOWLEDGE

Resurrection into an immortal person, which is Spiritually One with the Holy Spirit of our GOD the Father and HIS Son Jesus Christ. This is the Superior Baptism for those who live by the New Covenant of the Spirit of Jesus Christ, which is the Chrism of the Chosen Ones by the anointing of the Holy Spirit, and by accepting the Spirit of our Lord Jesus Christ and keeping His commands.

This dream I had explains my own Spiritual journey's past, present, and future, with the foreknowledge of a journey I hadn't completed yet, which is an explanation of the journey in this Earthly Realm that I was following. It was being revealed to me as a dream-vision that would become a revelation for me in order to keep my Spirit strong in faith as a Chosen Spiritual One living in Complete Unity.

The understanding of visions, dreams, signs, symbols, sounds, vibrations, spirits, and realms cannot be forced because they are tied into everything that you have been, are, and will become at the same time. If you are seeking the truth in your life for the meaning of that which you are gifted with while living in the Spirit, it will be revealed to you much easier because of your paying attention to it and having the Holy Spirit guiding you to the knowledge of the truth. The revelations will be understood by three reference points of past, present, and future, as you will see yourself in all three for understanding the direction that your Spiritual path is leading you on your journey. That will be proof to you that it is happening for a reason to bring you closer to our GOD the Father, where nothing will ever hold you back from HIM, HIS Word, and HIS love for you.

The meaning of this vision-dream for me in the "Spirit Realm" was an abbreviated version of my understanding as to how I was taught to view my own existence of the past, present, and future up to that point. I was being briefed to understand the direction I was being led by knowing where I first came from in my beginning as a reference point.

Firstly, my Spirit was created to appear in a place where I did not exist before and my eyes were open to see where I was for the first time. The darkness around me could not have produced me or anything of matter because it has no order of any life or anything of substance in it. I was created into existence by the Spirit power of my GOD the Father through my Lord Jesus Christ like a living Light Force of Spirit without the form of a body that I could actually see because I was only emitting light. The only thing I knew was that I came into existence instantly and had to find the purpose of my life. When I saw the entryway to the place I had to go to, it was the first thing that I had ever seen other than the darkness and the glow of my own existence. When I entered through the doorway into that creation, I knew I wasn't alone anymore. There was a Holy Spirit with me that was good and that taught me things, like the others who were created and had arrived long before me. They had their own Spirit in themselves that was once like mine before they arrived there.

Then I became aware that I was Spirit, neither male nor female, before I was placed in a male body. I noticed that I was clothed in a body which proved that this place I had entered was the Earthly Realm of matter where people lived in ignorance of the truth by forgetting where they came from and what they were created from. The Holy Spirit told me that I shouldn't desire to stay there, or I would become blind to the truth like the people who accept that realm of the worldly ways, and that I might never find my way out, so I had to leave right away.

I felt the sorrow in that realm because it is the realm of living in the past that is constantly passing away by time until it has ended in the death of the body and Spirit for those who don't have the help to escape it. No one there was living for the future; they only lived with their minds focused on the past as soon as they saw what they experienced in the present. That thought of a useless existence without escape is insanity. I wanted to help those that were there to have a way to escape it and for them to have eternal life in the Spirit Realm of the future that is not created to pass away by time. But I didn't know how to help them, and I needed to find a way to do that so they wouldn't have to die like everything else in that realm which is transitory; that is, it will all end someday.

Then, the Holy Spirit reminded me that I couldn't go backwards the way that I came through from the past and into this present Earthly Realm because there were no answers for me there or in the darkness. I had to find the answers I needed by using what I knew and what I would find out as the way to the future Spirit Realm for eternal life. By realizing where I was at that time, I became aware that I could move forward and search for a way that leads to a future with eternal life, not only for myself, but for others to know too.

So, I searched outside through the windows of that place, as if I began to search through the windows of my mind, and I saw a ledge which appeared to me in my mind to be the reflection of a narrow path for a Spiritual journey in search of the truth that leads to eternal life. The ledge was a difficult path to stay on if I didn't remain Spiritually focused and in complete control of my Body-Temple that I was just learning to live in. My body felt that this path was unnecessary and dangerous, but I was told that if I reacted to the emotions I felt in my body, it might get nervous and misstep or try to get off the Spiritual path, possibly causing it and my Spirit to both fall to death. If I fell to my death, all my hope would be lost by my failure to stay committed to living in the Spirit.

I was told that I had to remain living consciously in Spirit to control my body and my mind to stay on the Spirit path so that the journey would lead me out of the Earthly Realm and into a Realm of the Spirit that I didn't know much about. I was in search of something in the Spirit Realm that would help enlighten me in the understanding of the truth for myself and others, but I did not exactly know what it was yet.

Once I came to the end of the Spiritual path and completed that Spiritual journey, I knew that it was possible to remain living in the Spirit and in control of my body if I continued to follow the guidance of the Holy Spirit that was leading me to eternal life. When I reached the entryway to the Spirit Realm, the Chosen Ones who were there prepared to help me opened the entryway to the Spirit Realm and welcomed me in.

I knew I had been anointed with eternal life because I had remained living in Spirit while I followed the guidance of the Holy Spirit. When I drank the Water of Life, everything in me became renewed, healthy, and full of life by the awareness of this gift of foreknowledge that the Holy Spirit gives me. The thing I had learned in the Spirit Realm was that I would receive confirmation by enlightenment at the time I met the Chosen Spiritual Ones when the vision-dream was fulfilled. It was at that time that the Holy Spirit told me that they were the Chosen Spiritual Ones who would care for me. The woman I met is the Chosen Spiritual Editor who would manifest the words into a book that I had written in prayer for over a year, as I was commanded to do, and I did it in good faith. Therefore, the Spiritual interpretation of the vision-dream was a revelation of the truth in my life to me.

The meaning of this vision-dream in the Earthly Realm of matter is a reflection of the Spiritual Realm. It started with my awareness that I was reminded of: that I knew I was in existence and that I could hear, but I could not see myself before I was born a baby. Before that, I was nothing. Then, as a child, the Holy Spirit told me that the body I was in was not really me; it was something that I am given to live within for this Earthly Realm while He was with me. I believed Him as a Child of Light living in my body. Then later, the Holy Spirit told me that I was speaking to Jesus Christ, who was also with me. He showed me that this realm had the evil of darkness in it that made people weak, fearful, sad, blind, hopeless, and fall into sin. They told me that I should not fear evil, but refuse it as I did when they showed me the spirit of darkness as a child in my room.

This was my Spiritual journey that I had to learn about and stay on. They showed me two Spirits, Angels with Robes of Light, who were with me to protect me from the evil spirits of darkness. This made my faith so strong that I would never be afraid of the darkness because my protection of my Lord Jesus Christ is the Living Spirit of Light that is in me, and I am in His Light.

FOREKNOWLEDGE

I had to learn about Spirits so I could become what I was being taught to be: a Chosen Spiritual One who is enlightened to understand the Word of Truth and bring it to the ones that need it so they may be able to recognize the lies of this world that hold them captive from going to our Almighty GOD the Father and becoming HIS Child of Light like I am, as I am living in Spirit and in Complete Unity. All those things are explained in the book, Inspiration For Your Eternal Life, that I was inspired to write and give to the Chosen Spiritual Editor that I had never met before that vision-dream.

All these things were part of helping me through the path of fulfilling the prophecy that I would bring the Word of Truth to people who are imprisoned. And by doing that, I would fulfill the prophecy which I was shown in a vision, that some day I would speak in front of an audience in the prison to explain how my Lord Jesus Christ helped me write His message to the world in a book, the way He taught me to understand who He is: the Son of our GOD the Father.

I made some phone calls to people I knew who had published books before, as I tried to find the editor I was supposed to meet. It took over a couple of months until I got an appointment and finally met her and her husband, who were the two persons in the Spirit Realm room of my vision-dream. We had lunch and I briefly told them about the dream I had and that it was being fulfilled as we spoke. It was a blessing to know that they were very excited to be part of my journey. I was told to let them know that when this book is published, it will rain, which means there will be many blessings to all those who read it to find the Word of Truth for their own eternal life that will stand the test of time. That explains why my gift of foreknowledge is essential for the interpretation of my vision-dream in the Spirit Realm and the Earthly Realm that reflect both sides of my life that become a revelation at the same time.

The message in the Word of Truth tells me not to live in the past, or I will be living in sorrow for things I cannot change, and that I must not wait with anxiety to be in the future of perfection, or I will not be prepared for the future. I must diligently seek and master the Word of Truth in the present as I live in the Spirit now to become prepared to move forward into the future Spirit Realm of perfection with the help of my Lord Jesus Christ for the refinement towards the perfection of my Spirit.

Throughout my prayers while authoring my book, I was led to the truth by the Holy Spirit about the creation of Adam, the first perfect man created in Spirit, then put in flesh, and how the descendants of Adam will be living in the New Covenant of the Spirit by proving their love for my GOD the Father and HIS Son my Lord Jesus Christ.

FOREKNOWLEDGE

First, we are all created in Spirit as a perfect Spirit from our GOD the Father and through HIS Son, our Lord Jesus Christ, to return to them as a recreated Holy Child Spirit. No one is born with sin, not of their own or another person. We are perfect until we sin on our own in this Earthly Realm. No one is responsible for our sins except ourselves. Adam paid for his own sin, and we must pay for our own as well.

Therefore, our GOD the Father gave us a gift to be free from sin and death by HIS New Covenant of the Spirit concerning HIS Son, our Lord Jesus Christ. By accepting HIS Son, our Lord Jesus Christ, and following His commands, we must repent our own sins to GOD the Father in the Name of HIS Son Jesus Christ and return to living a Holy Life now. We are Spiritual Children of GOD the Father who recreates us through HIS Son Jesus Christ, who gives us the Chrism of the Child, which is our resurrection of eternal life in the flesh now, to be redeemed after the death of our Body-Temple when we are raised up by the Holy Spirit and transformed into an incorruptible Spirit-Body with eternal life. This is the foreknowledge of our future that all the faithful Chosen Ones will believe in without a doubt or fear.

Second, we are expected to know our own testimony of sanctification and salvation in detail as a witness in our own minds to be reminded of our struggles and enlightenment to keep our own faith strong by the memory of the love of our GOD the Father and HIS Son Jesus Christ, as we learned from the Holy Spirit all the truth in our lifetime now. We should make a record of everything we can remember to contemplate it until the truth of it is written in our hearts. This is how we will become mature in Spirit as Chosen Spiritual Ones. It takes courage and effort to honestly do such a thing. The cowardly, lazy, lacking in faith, and liars will have trouble with it, but unless they come to terms and humble themselves to my GOD the Father through my Lord Jesus Christ, they will lose everything and everyone they ever loved by their own judgment.

This is exactly what the enlightenment of foreknowledge brings to those who are Chosen Ones. It's the Word of GOD through HIS Son Jesus Christ who speaks to us in many languages of symbols, signs, sounds, dreams, visions, vibrations and an infinite number of ways for each of us to learn that our GOD the Father is calling us to HIMSELF through HIS Son our Lord Jesus Christ who tells the Holy Spirit what we must do and say.

We are in the beginning of our own creation since the powerful angel spirits that were supposed to care for mankind deceived the first ones by a lie, which was as sinful transgression against our GOD the Father. They knew it would lead to their doom and destruction of their spirit for committing the transgression. Nevertheless, our ancestors made a decision to

FOREKNOWLEDGE

believe the sinful lie and also transgress against the Word of our GOD the Father. Since they were deceived by a higher power, they were placed into flesh that would die. And they were to live out their lives to repent their sin and ask to be forgiven for what they had done. The meaning of our life now is to decide to have life or reject life and remain in the condition that we are first created Spirit in flesh that will die like everything else in the world including the earth, or decide to except eternal life by living in the Covenant of the Spirit with our Lord Jesus Christ who gives us life in our recreation to live in Complete Unity with Him and our GOD the Father who gives us HIS Holy Spirit to guide us with Foreknowledge.

We are not of this world, which is transitory, and we must become who and what we are supposed to be as HIS Children of Light. We must become refined to enlightenment by living in our Spirit and having our Lord Jesus Christ to be anointed with the Holy Spirit and Fire from our GOD the Father. We are constantly being refined towards Spiritual perfection every day to become and remain perfect with the gift of foreknowledge as help from our Lord Jesus Christ within us. Foreknowledge is a gift of Spiritual Grace for enlightenment with eternal life that we are glorified with by our GOD the Father and through our Lord Jesus Christ, as we all live for our GOD the Father through our Lord Jesus Christ and with the Holy Spirit as One.

Chapter 18 - The Image of Creation

It had taken over fifty years for me to have been gifted with the confirmation that my GOD the Father is far greater than all creation, and that no word in creation can utter HIS Name. In other words, anything that can be said in any way is not enough to personify HIS True Entity. HE has created my Lord Jesus Christ to become HIS first and only created Son, as the greatest of all creation. His given Name, Jesus Christ, personifies the Son of the Living GOD the Father, who has given the power over all creation to HIS Christ with that Name He was given. By His Name of power, He purifies all creation from error, darkness, evil, and corruption by suffering through death for us willingly, as our GOD the Father sent Him to do by HIS will to give us eternal life. Since His death and Resurrection from the Cross, my Lord Jesus Christ is making all things new and perfect, including His Chosen Ones, who He will call up to Himself at their appointed time on the last day.

I consider myself to be grateful for His blessings, and as a Chosen One, to see the mystery of creation and to have come to an understanding of it with His guidance through the Holy Spirit that I am One with in Spirit. I will be the first to say that it was a gift that I accepted at a very young age and have watched over it in my mind throughout my life as I waited patiently for the interpretation of its meanings for over fifty years. I cannot and do not ever wish to boast about that; I only appreciate that I was the Chosen Spiritual One to deliver this message to share with the people of the world who will decide to believe and follow our Lord Jesus Christ and His commands for Eternal Life.

Our Lord Jesus Christ created our first ancestor of humankind in the Image of GOD, and we are the offspring. The image in which man was made for this realm is also the image of all creation, which was created with our Spirit through our Lord Jesus Christ by GOD and formed together with a body of flesh that is made for this Earth Realm in which we occupy at any given time that HE allows us to dwell in, by HIS will.

Our very Center, where there can be no more center than the very Center, is where our Spirit of Life that we were recreated with, rests within our Body-Temple Holiest Place. It is within our holiest place, referred to the same as the Holy Temple "Bridal Chamber", the Kingdom of Heaven, which is the heart of our Spirit dwelling. When we learn to believe and commit ourselves through our Lord Jesus Christ to our GOD the Father, we are joined with the Holy Spirit that comes out of our GOD the Father, and the Spirit of our Lord Jesus Christ, and the Spirit of GOD the Father that can dwell with HIS fullness in HIS Son our Lord Jesus Christ, all three in our Holy of Holiest place with our Spirit

THE IMAGE OF CREATION

within us as One. That is the place where we are joined together within our Body-Temple to remain Holy in Complete Unity with them. Therefore, we can see ourselves as the fourth person in the Kingdom of Heaven within us. Our center place is the entry to the Kingdom of Heaven for our Resurrection to eternal life and a place of Holiness where we are constantly being filled by the power of the Holy Spirit from our God the Father through our Lord Jesus Christ, to be continuously refined to purity and perfection as a Child of GOD. This is how we live by Spirit now in Complete Unity with them for eternal life.

Before my GOD the Father commanded a Temple to be built in the wilderness, HE rested on Mount Sinai after HE came down in a Pillar of Fire and spoke with Moses in front of the Israelites when they settled in the desert wilderness after being led out of captivity from Egypt. Here is the descriptive comparison of our Body-Temple to the Holy Temple that our GOD the Father instructed the Israelites to build with perimeter walls around the Temple itself, which was made in the symbol of creation. There were two main sections within the temple: the Holiest Place and the Holy Place. A large Curtain barrier, sixty feet high by thirty feet wide and approximately four inches thick, covered the entrance of the Holiest Place in the Temple, separating it from the Holy Place in the Temple. The Holiest Place in the Temple is where the Spirit from our GOD the Father would meet with a single Priest for the Israelites every year. It is also called the Bridal Chamber, where the Spirit of our GOD the Father would come together with the people to be in accord with them. He would meet with them according to the Old Covenant of that time. Sometimes the Angel Gabriel that stood in the presence of my GOD the Father would be present in the Holiest Place to give whatever message necessary at that time. The Holy Place was made up of the larger portion of the two main temple rooms. Those two main chambers together made up the largest dwelling areas of the Temple. Then they placed the outer surrounding perimeter walls at a distance from the Temple at the north, south, east, and west directions.

The Center Place of our Body-Temple, which is the same as the Bridal Chamber and the Holiest Place within us, is where we become One in Complete Unity to be with our GOD the Father, HIS Son our Lord Jesus Christ, the Holy Spirit, and our Personal Spirit as the fourth One. This is our portal to the Kingdom of Heaven. As a Chosen One, I see myself as the fourth One in the Kingdom of Heaven as my Lord Jesus Christ taught me; the Kingdom of Heaven is within me, and blessed is the one who sees themself as the fourth One in the Kingdom of Heaven.

From the outside of the Holiest Place within us, the rest of our body within us is the larger Holy Place in our Body-Temple, which completes our form as our Body-Temple. The outer form of our Body-Temple is the final,

THE IMAGE OF CREATION

complete image of the Temple of GOD, positioned within the exterior surrounding perimeter walls. From our Body-Temple form to the exterior surrounding perimeter walls is all creation, that is the boundary that contains the area of all creation, and it contains this entire Realm of Matter that surrounds us and all created space at a distance from us until there is no more creation. On the outside of the exterior surrounding perimeter boundary walls, which contain all the existing space and creation, there is complete darkness, nothingness, lifelessness, and without the Light of Creation. That is the image of all creation in which the first man was made Holy in nature and without darkness or sin. We are His offspring made in the Image of GOD, made the same way as all creation, which is an image reflection of GOD, but is not GOD the Father HIMSELF.

At the beginning of creation, there was Spirit and Water, the two substances we must also have within our body, or our flesh cannot become a living soul. My Lord Jesus Christ taught me that I must become Spirit and Water as it was in the beginning. Water is also like Spirit; it is alive. Therefore, my Lord Jesus Christ removed evil from water on Earth to sanctify our water for our repentance to remove evil from our Body-Temple. That was what the baptism of John the Baptist symbolized by the asking of our GOD the Father in repentance to remove our sin in Spirit prayer and cleanse our Spirit, Water, and Blood internally from sin at that time. It also symbolized a commitment to keep HIS commands from that time forward in our lives on earth. It did not give anyone the Holy Spirit before our Lord Jesus Christ died on the Crucifix, and since my Lord Jesus Christ had not risen from the dead, He had not returned to my GOD the Father yet to ask Him to send us HIS Holy Spirit into us as our guide to the truth. Even so, on and so forth, the Baptism of John is for repentance even to this day.

Under the New Covenant of the Spirit of my Lord Jesus Christ, we are sanctified within our body temple now by believing and following the commands of my Lord Jesus Christ by living in the Spirit that is controlling our Body-Temple's flesh and mind. We can only do this by living by the commands of my Lord Jesus Christ to be ready for His sanctification when He sees that we have the will to receive eternal life by accepting His Spirit of life living in us as one. Only by the help of having our Lord Jesus Christ with His Spirit of Life within us, will the Holy Spirit of our GOD the Father come into us to live within us and guide us in Complete Unity.

We were made perfect in Spirit without sin in any way, and we lived that way as a child. When each of us committed sin, we were separated from the Spirit of GOD the Father by that sin. The Holy Spirit does not dwell in a place with sin, and that is what a person gives up when they choose to sin again and the Holy Spirit leaves them by the choice of that person to live with sin in themselves. HE loved us as a child and loves us now; it is HIS will for us to return to HIM with HIS Holy Spirit and to become a perfect Holy Spirit again as a Child of GOD. That is why HE sent our Lord Jesus Christ to help us do just that. If we had no sin, He would not have come here to this Earthly Realm to offer us His salvation from that condemnation that leads to the Second Death, which is the doom and destruction of our personal Spirit by our own judgment not to accept HIS gift of Life and to remain in sin.

My Lord Jesus Christ gives us the Chrism of the Holy Spirit for salvation, which is the Superior Baptism. That is what He did for the man He forgave, who was put to death on the crucifix next to Him. The man was in paradise with my Lord Jesus Christ that day. No dipping in the water was necessary before he received the Holy Spirit because he asked for salvation and received it right then on the cross while he was still alive, and after our Lord Jesus Christ had already died on the cross and was glorified in Spirit at once by our GOD the Father. My Lord Jesus Christ is Lord over the Chrism, and He has given His Chrism to me when I was a child to recreate me into a Spirit Child of our GOD the Father. It is His choice by His will to give the gift of life the way He desires to give it to each person. I don't live by the traditions of man, but by the Truth in the Word of my GOD the Father with HIS Son, my Lord Jesus Christ. That has been my belief since I was five years old when I naturally accepted Him to live as One within me.

VINCENTE GARCIA

The Temple of my GOD the Father, is a Holy Realm on Earth that would be occupied by the Holy Spirit of my GOD the Father. That is why it has perimeter walls separating it from the rest of creation. As my Lord Jesus Christ taught me that the entire world is condemned to destruction, and I must not be part of it in my Spirit, heart, or mind, or I will be subject to the same fate of destruction.

The Holy Temple Bridal Chamber, which was built from stone and called the Temple of Solomon in Jerusalem, was destroyed in 587 BCE before my Lord Jesus Christ came to Earth in the flesh. The Ark of the Covenant was saved with all the things that were in the Bridal Chamber. They were taken out from the Holy of Holies by an Angel of GOD, to include the Large Curtain that separated everything in the Holy of Holies from the larger chamber called the Holy Place. They were placed underground, where the Earth opened and swallowed them, outside of the Northern Exterior perimeter wall where there is a Northern Gate called the Damascus Gate and a hill called Golgotha or Skull Hill, which is where my Lord Jesus Christ was put to death on the Crucifix over the Ark of the Covenant. The Ark of the Covenant was placed in the Earth by an Angel of GOD because the Old Covenant was not completed, and the Ark of the Covenant was also being preserved underground in a cave under Golgotha for the final Sacrificial Lambs Sacred Blood to be sprinkled onto the Western side of the Ark of the Covenant. His Sacred blood from His wounds flowed down the Crucifix and onto the Mercy Seat, through the cracks in the rocks above where the Ark of the Covenant was, where it was preserved by Angels of GOD for the Blood of the Messiah, our Lord Jesus Christ. Therefore, after His Sacred Blood ran into the earth, He said on the cross, "It is finished."

After Solomon's Temple was destroyed, another temple was built in its place and called the Temple of Herod, which had another Curtain made to separate the two Chambers. The Curtain in the Temple of Herod was destroyed by Michael the Archangel of GOD who cut it in two from top to bottom with his Flaming Sword that extended from his hand, when my Lord Jesus Christ was on the cross. The Stone Temples are no longer needed for the New Covenant of the Spirit of my Lord Jesus Christ, which is now in effect in our hearts. So, the animals of flesh sacrifices are no longer needed since the sacrifice of my Lord Jesus Christ was the final and Superior Sacrifice with His human flesh, blood, and water. And now the New Covenant of the Spirit of our Lord Jesus Christ brings eternal life to all those who believe in Him and accept His Chrism of the Spirit into our heart, the Bridal Chamber, our Center place to become One with Him. Sacrifices are no longer needed to be done by us because there is no sacrifice better than our Lord Jesus Christ, who died once and for all to be forgiven for our sins.

So we have the image of the Cross in our heart, mind, and Spirit, that brings us understanding of what it means for us and all creation to the point of enlightenment to receive the Light of the Holy Spirit, which gives us the Resurrection for Eternal Life now, so we may be Redeemed after the death of our Body-Temple and be transformed into Spirit-Bodies like our Lord Jesus Christ is Spirit.

After our Lord Jesus Christ's death, and while His Body-Temple was on the Crucifix, He retrieved the Holy Spiritual Ones from the bondage of sin in the Realm of Hell through the opened portal of the Holy of Holiest place. The Spirit of my GOD the Father no longer dwells in a temple of stone after the last Temple Curtain was torn in two from top to bottom by the Archangel Michael, who has a Flaming Sword that extends from His hand. Michael was there with His Angels to worship our Lord Jesus Christ when our Lord Jesus Christ was crucified and died on the cross to destroy the power of death, evil, and the bondage of sin in the darkness of the Realm of Hell over Humanity that kept their Spirits from returning to our GOD the Father in Paradise.

The symbolic renting of the curtain in two, from top to bottom, signified the Spiritual opening of the portal that links Under Earth, this Earthly Realm, to the Kingdom of Heaven for safe passage to enter the Kingdom of Heaven as a Holy Child of GOD and to become One with HIM through our Lord Jesus Christ. It is the same

THE IMAGE OF CREATION

as our Lord Jesus Christ removing the veil that covers the face of anyone who reads the Mosaic Law in the Old Covenant from seeing the truth in the Word of GOD, so they may see the Truth in Him and know who He is: The Son of our GOD the Father and the Son is our Lord and Savior. Only now our Lord Jesus Christ anoints us with the Holy Spirit of our GOD the Father within our Body-Temple for us to become One with them in our Holiest Place. Which is the Bridal Chamber in our Heart where we become One in Complete Unity. That is exactly what He had prayed for that day to our GOD the Father, just before He was crucified to die and be raised from the dead by the Holy Spirit of our GOD the Father. Three days later, He reappeared in the flesh to prove that He was resurrected by the Holy Spirit of our GOD the Father.

The vision of the Lion Spirit in a park that I interacted with as a child was given to me at a young age to remember all of my life, and is also a reminder for me to remember the Image of Creation. My Lord Jesus Christ made it for me to understand by experiencing the way to salvation through Him, with Him, and in Him as One in Spirit. He let me see myself as One in His Spirit with Him and I felt His perfect love completely through me in a sense that cannot be explained by words. It has to be experienced to understand how it fulfills the Spirit within us completely. I have now learned to understand that the vision is for all the Chosen Children of our GOD the Father that are being called to HIMSELF, through our Lord Jesus Christ, to know that by His blood sacrifice He will cleanse us and all creation from all sin in existence. Everyone must know that He has already made that sacrifice and the cleansing is happening now. This is the New Covenant of the Spirit by my Lord Jesus Christ, who was sent to save the Chosen Spiritual Ones who accept Him now to become Resurrected to eternal life within their Body-Temple before it dies.

At first, in my youth, my Lord Jesus Christ watched me to see which toy animal figurine I liked most of all as I listened to the radio, and He saw that I favored the lion. He knew that I had listened to His voice before and that I would recognize it again; I only needed to know who was speaking to me by His Name Jesus. Then He made sure that I would accept Him this way by knowing I could speak to Him and He would speak to me by calling me through my mind with telepathy from the direction of the Sacred Heart Tapestry hanging on the wall behind me. I never thought for a second that the tapestry had powers; it never felt that way, yet I knew that He was with me and had spoken to me at the age of five before I ever saw the tapestry on the wall. It was just a way for me to know that He is always with me, while He was drawing my attention to the picture that looked like Him so I would know what He looked like. I felt that He was alive with me and not in the Sacred Heart Tapestry.

THE IMAGE OF CREATION

He sent His Angels to appear to me dressed in Robes of Light when I was alone in my room at night because I had become aware that dark spirits were trying to get to me from the darkness. Knowing that the Angels were with me would allow me to rest as their Robes of Light were like a night light that repelled evil and darkness from within me and outside of me, and that made me fearless of the darkness for the rest of my life. The Angels spoke to me by telepathy, allowing me to rest as they faced away from me so I would not be nervous about their faces looking at me while I laid down to sleep. I became familiar with the Light of Life, which was emitting a vibration that gave me a feeling of love and peace that felt like it was completely caressing me inside and out. The Angels allowed me to sit up in my bed close to them to see their Robes of Light up close with my own eyes to see that the Light was alive and was flowing with life. It reminded me of the word "beautiful" to see it react in awareness to my presence as I looked at it. That's when I knew that the Spirit of Life and Light was with me and that evil things could not get to me because the power of the Living Light that is from my GOD the Father is my protection.

With all these visions and the showing of Himself to me by all these diverse ways through my Lord Jesus Christ, I was motivated to follow the Holy Spirit, and I had the will to worship my GOD the Father in Spirit by praying and singing in praises to HIM in Church at that time. By learning all these things this way, I had accepted to believe in Him, and I accepted Him to be One with me before I ever owned or read a bible when I was between the ages of five and ten.

The keyword is I "believe" in Him and love Him with all my heart, mind, and Spirit, which is all of my existence. Everything I learned by listening to my Lord Jesus Christ through the Holy Spirit made me sanctified enough to be ready to find a deeper meaning of how He speaks to me in whispers, symbols, signs, sounds, dreams, visions, vibrations, which I recognized to be a language specifically tailored for my understanding of the truth. This is why He showed me the next Image of Creation to contemplate in patience, faith, power, and self-control throughout my life for the answers that were to be revealed to me after I became mature in Spirit and when I was ready to accept them. These are revelations for the Chosen Ones to have an understanding of the Truth of the Word without doubt or fear. The Word can speak in any language at any time; He is all languages, known and hidden.

The image of the Lion was for me to be comfortable with seeing Him in Spirit and to know that I must not fear anything, including the Image of the Spirit, living in Spirit, or speaking of the Spirit Realm at any time, because I am Spirit too. I must remember that everything that my Lord Jesus Christ shows me through the Holy Spirit is for myself to understand and to help others understand its meaning. By His voice, I knew it

THE IMAGE OF CREATION

was Him appearing in the form of a Lion, and it never crossed my mind as odd because I know He is capable of doing anything. I knew there was a reason for it. That reason would be revealed to me when it was time for me to know. I had already accepted that as how He would always communicate with me specifically, and how I would understand what He is communicating to me by our relationship. His voice is a vibration that comforts me and gives me peace, and I know His voice just like I know the voice of anyone else I love.

The image of the eye of the Spirit Lion was reflecting the image of salvation for those who are being called to my GOD the Father. The outer black line on the exterior of the eye was the darkness of nothingness that surrounds all creation. The golden iris that glowed by the Living Light of the eye is the Chosen Ones that are being called from the world by my GOD the Father, they are all being purified and refined into perfection like the finest and brightest gold that glows with the Light of Life from within it. We are being constantly purified by the Holy Spirit and Fire, who is constantly guiding us and caring for us in every way possible with love, tenderness, and truth from our Lord Jesus Christ. Being within the center of the eye within the Light of Life showed me that I am one with the Living Light of Life in the Spirit. I am in Him, and He is in me, and there is nothing that this Eye of Light could not see in me or that I could not see in its entirety by all my senses and thoughts, so nothing at all can be hidden from the truth between us all. I was allowed to move freely into the body of my Lord Jesus Christ at will, and He never resisted me seeking the truth in Him to satisfy all of my questions and curiosities to know Him thoroughly. He did not turn me away from any truth because His will is the will of my GOD the Father: to bring all that are called to HIM without fail.

The Body of my Lord Jesus Christ has ample room for all creation to remain within Him. He is the Church for the first man and all of his offspring that are Chosen Ones to remain attached to our Lord Jesus Christ for eternal life. The Blood Red Fire that covered both of His eyes is the symbol of the New Covenant of the Spirit that actively cleanses all creation of sin and evil since the Blood Sacrifice that He shed on the Cross, which covers all creation and darkness. He is our Lord over all, who is Superior to all things by the power and authority of my GOD the Father. Only through having Him with us in Complete Unity will we live alive now by being Resurrected before our Body-Temple dies. We will then be raised up by the Holy Spirit that is One with our Spirit through that death to bring us up to see the redemption and transformation into an eternal Spirit-Body to enter the Kingdom of my GOD the Father and to be with HIM. This is how, to this day, my Lord Jesus Christ is still fulfilling the will of my GOD the Father for us through the Holy Spirit.

THE IMAGE OF CREATION

By understanding to believe that we were created in the image of our GOD the Father through HIS Son, our Lord Jesus Christ, and by HIS mercy that we were given the gift of life as we honor HIS Son, we can receive the Chrism of the Holy Spirit from our GOD the Father through accepting to have our Lord Jesus Christ at this time. HIS Holy Spirit is HIS deposit actively living within HIS Chosen Ones as a promise for us to be redeemed into eternal perfection for the next Realm of the Spirit. It is HIS choice for us to have eternal life, and our decision to accept HIS gift of eternal life through having HIS Son, Jesus Christ.

That is why our Lord Jesus Christ taught us to keep HIS commands: to show that we love Him and each other as brothers and sisters. Our Lord Jesus Christ will take us all with Him to instantly appear in the presence of our GOD the Father to be given a higher grace of perfection, which HE intended for us to become enlightened in Spirit before the beginning of creation.

Only then by HIS will, will the Chosen Ones receive the Crown of Righteousness as a gift, which is another Chrism for us to be fully anointed in Spirit with Forethought, Foreknowledge, Eternal Life, Incorruptibility, and Truth to live forever as One with them, just like our Lord Jesus Christ was created perfect by our GOD the Father to live as One with our GOD the Father before the creation of anything else. Then we will be taken to live in our new home in the New

VINCENTE GARCIA

Kingdom, conjoined with a New Earth and New Heaven with them in the Spirit Realm of Perfection.

Our Lord Jesus Christ speaks to us through the Holy Spirit in whispers, images, signs, symbols, sounds, visions, dreams, vibrations, and many other diverse ways that trigger our minds to become clear to understand the hidden truths of creation that will be in our minds and believed in our hearts forever. Sometimes knowledge is passed to me without having to ask for it because the Holy Spirit that always searches my heart knows what I need before I know I have the need to ask for it. My trust in my GOD the Father has moved to a higher Spiritual level of understanding that HE will fulfill all my needs without fail because HE loves me. I am HIS, now and forever.

It was brought to my attention after a vision-dream that I had a question in my mind that I needed to be answered for my heart to become fully content by Spiritual knowledge, and I didn't quite know I needed to know it the way I know the answer now. This is what I saw and what it means to me now from the time I woke up from the dream with a more powerful faith in my Lord Jesus Christ to help make my faith spiritually perfect.

In this vision-dream, I was standing in the middle of a room in my castle, dressed in a thick, colorful robe and enjoying the comfort of the fire coming from my fireplace that was seven feet tall and ten feet wide. This is the castle that I had built for my protection from the forces of evil. The walls were made of the hardest stone known to man and were at least fifteen feet thick. There was one door that led into another room where there were many guards lounging and resting until I needed something. Then I heard the voice of the Holy Spirit tell me that the demons are going to enter the castle through the hidden imperfections in the walls. As soon as I heard His voice, I listened for the demons and heard many of them trying to get into my room through the walls. They were well prepared and dressed in full armor with every weapon to attack me at a time I wasn't wearing my armor.

I heard the voice of the Holy Spirit tell me in haste to call for help. So, I hurried to the door of the guards room and yelled, "the demons are coming" but there was no response. The voice of the Holy Spirit told me to yell louder, so I cracked the door open and yelled, "We are being attacked." Still, there was no response. Then I heard the Holy Spirit tell me again in a firm voice to yell louder, so I opened the door all the way and yelled with everything I had, "The demons are attacking through the walls!" Then I saw the mighty Angels of my GOD rise up in full armor and surround me to protect me from the attacking demons. They fought so fiercely with each other that I couldn't tell who was going to win at first, until I noticed that the Angels were not fighting as hard as they could. They were only keeping the demons away from me to show me something. As I was protected in the middle of a ring of Angels surrounding me, I noticed one of the Angels take hold of a demon and dragged it into the flames of fire in the fireplace. The Angel was continuously looking at me as if He wanted me to watch Him control the resisting demon in the fire. As the Angel was sitting on the large burning wood pile, still controlling the demon, the Angel appeared to change into a second Spirit form inside of His own form. His outer form was translucent, so I could see that He had two forms as One. The form inside of Him was another Spirit with the power of Death. The Angel made sure I was watching what He was doing when He stuck His tongue out of his mouth and effortlessly touched the demon on its shoulder armor with His tongue. Then instantly, all the demons in the room vanished where they stood like they never existed. Everything was quiet as the rest of the Angels around me returned to their resting places.

I was amazed as the Angel in the fire lounged comfortably over the large burning logs stacked in the fireplace. Then I noticed that the Angel was dressed in a Robe of Light with His hands and bare feet exposed, and when I took a closer look at His face, I knew He was my Lord Jesus Christ. As soon as I looked at His bare feet again, He said these words for me to remember forever: "My feet were made to follow the will of GOD." As soon as I heard Him speak those words, it was set in my mind to give me a new mindset: His mindset. The change in my mind happened to take away the unfocused parts of my thoughts to bring me clarity of the Truth in the Word to become who I am supposed to be like. My vision started to fade as I was waking up from the vivid vision-dream. I knew exactly what everything meant with the last words that He spoke, still echoing in my mind and being repeated carefully and clearly by the Holy Spirit over and over again as it echoed in my mind for me to remember when I became wide awake. When I became awake, I started to speak those words as I repeated the words out loud to myself, "My feet were made to follow the will of GOD." I thought to write it down, until I realized, "How could I ever forget it?"

The knowledge of Spiritual power comes from understanding the things we are shown and putting them into practice when necessary. By that, we are defined by the things we actually believe, do, and say. As a Chosen One, I believe and live by the New Covenant of the Spirit, knowing that my feet were made to follow the will of GOD.

To first understand this vision-dream that my Lord Jesus Christ showed me, I am compelled to remember what I am doing and that I am doing it through my Lord Jesus Christ for my GOD the Father, without fear or doubt to give glory to my GOD the Father.

VINCENTE GARCIA

Then I knew the stone construction of my castle walls are the building blocks with each day of my lifetime in Spiritual belief. In that belief, I cannot leave any day hidden in the secret spaces in my mind, which are weak points for demons to enter through in my mind. Every stone is a thought that must be solid and purely formed with the love of my GOD the Father. Every stone, which is a thought in my mind that appears to have spaces or cracks, must be discarded and replaced with solid thoughts that conform to the standards of the Word of Truth. Because the weakest thoughts of the mind lead to sin, where the demons will tempt and attack the mind if the Word of Truth is not put in its place to become a defense for that weakness.

The Angel of GOD was actually my Lord Jesus Christ, who was showing me the power of the tongue, which is like a two-edged sword against the power of evil when I use the Word of Truth to resist them. No demon has the power to fight against the Word of Truth any more than any human. The best they can do is tell people it is not true to get them not to go to our Lord Jesus Christ for sanctification and salvation from the death they wish upon us to deprive our GOD the Father of our love for HIM. They want people to fear and doubt our relationship with our GOD the Father, as they enjoy pretending that they have power over people. Truly, the best they can do is take the weak people with them to the second death of their spirit that they know will happen to their own spirit at their own appointed time.

THE IMAGE OF CREATION

Two men who were possessed by a legion of demons once admitted that they knew they had an appointed time for destruction as they spoke to my Lord Jesus Christ before He sent them into a herd of pigs, and the pigs all drowned themselves in water. That is a warning to the world of what will happen to those who do not have the Holy Spirit and my Lord Jesus Christ in Complete Unity.

When any weakness of my mind is discovered, and temptation appears, I must call for the help of my Lord Jesus Christ in Spiritual prayer to my GOD the Father to glorify HIM with my entire existence like my life depends on it by those exigent circumstances. A Child of Light must constantly strive to rid themself of anything that causes them to have weakness in the Spiritual walls of defense from evil. By calling on my GOD the Father in the Name of my Lord Jesus Christ, He will send His Angels directly to help me.

As Enlightened Children of GOD, we must remember the very first command is to love GOD with all our heart, mind, and Spirit in Spirit prayer. With that belief, we must understand that we are servants of our GOD the Father because HE created us. Therefore, we are recreated to do HIS will without doubt or fear. And the very last words my Lord Jesus Christ taught me in this vision-dream were to remember that my feet were made to follow the will of GOD. And as long as I adhere to the Word of Truth, I will remain in the love of my GOD the Father, the same as my Lord Jesus Christ has done with the Incorruptible Spirit that He is in me, His Chosen Spiritual One.

All these things are intended for me as a Chosen One to understand in a language that only I could learn throughout my lifetime, to understand His way of speaking to me, so that I will continue believing in the truth to become enlightened in Spirit perfection. We are created in the Image of GOD by HIS creation through HIS Son Jesus Christ, who is all things, including the Lord of all creation. As a Chosen Spiritual One, I must become One with Him in His image and His Spirit nature, starting now. By remaining in Him, I will learn how to become mature in the Spirit for eternal life. This is my will for all my brothers and sisters that have been Chosen: to become One in the image of my Lord Jesus Christ, who is the First Creation in the image of Life for eternity, and who was created by my GOD the Father in HIS image and nature as HIS only begotten Son. My Lord Jesus Christ has recreated my Spirit in His nature and in His image, which is symbolically the image of creation and spiritually the image and nature of my GOD the Father. Therefore, we can be One in Spirit with them as we are recreated with them in Complete Unity.

Chapter 19 - From GOD

There is a definitive decision that we all have to come to terms with at some point in our lives, as we know it, and with that decision, we will have been brought to an understanding that we cannot live without the mercy of someone taking the time to care for us because we cannot live without help. An example for the proof of that is: the help we needed at the beginning of our lives on earth to have been able to survive up to the point where we were able to provide for ourselves living in the society that we are subject to in the present day. By that, everyone has been given an opportunity to realize that we need each other to take care of each other as a family living as One.

But as it is, we become confused by the world and soon forget that we need each other and slowly become dull when our memory fails us after we are overcome by the desires of the flesh and the distractions of this world. The condemned people learn to live with sin by becoming selfish. That is why my Lord Jesus Christ taught me that it is essential to become enlightened by the Word of Truth by keeping the commands of our GOD the Father that were given to us through my Lord Jesus Christ. And by His Body Sacrificial Death our flesh is cleansed to accept the Holy Spirit of Fire and the Spirit of Life which our GOD the Father put in HIS Son, our Lord Jesus Christ. We also receive the Holy

Spirit which is the Spirit of Truth that comes out of our GOD the Father and into us to lead us to the Truth. Finally, we must receive the Spirit of Incorruptibility from our Lord Jesus Christ by remaining with Him, which is why we must remain attached to Him like a vine branch attached to the vine to stay alive. My Lord Jesus Christ is the Eternal Life with Incorruptibility, Truth, Forethought, and Foreknowledge. We must become like Him by having Him with us at all times, as we are One with Him.

Your definitive decision will be the last decision you will ever decide as one who is living condemned to eternal death in this Earth Realm. At the time of that one decision is the time when you will have found the end of your life in the flesh of the living dead, and you will have found the beginning of your new Spirit life living alive in the Spirit with eternal life for the Spirit Realm. It will be your first step that you will have taken to start living your eternal life as a living Chosen Spiritual One, a Child of GOD. This is the Crossing Over from death to life, which ultimately means that you are blessed by our GOD the Father from the very first step you take towards HIM by believing in HIS Son, our Lord Jesus Christ, and keeping His commands living by the Spirit in the New Covenant of the Spirit of our Lord Jesus Christ. That is the Testimony of our GOD the Father.

The definitive decision is to accept the gift of eternal life by accepting to believe in my GOD the Father through

HIS Son, Jesus Christ, who will give you the Chrism of HIS Holy Spirit to help you understand the Word of Truth to become refined as One in Complete Unity with them. Our Lord Jesus Christ is actively living in the Chosen Ones, and is actively teaching us to know Himself and our GOD the FATHER every moment of our lives as we pay attention to Him and keep His commands without fear or doubt.

This is the Word of GOD and HIS Covenant of the Spirit that HE has made as a choice for us to live in the Spirit Realm for eternal life with HIM. No one else had anything to do with making this choice for us, so no one can say they can do this themselves without help. This choice was given to us as a gift by the mercy and from the love of our GOD the Father, who is love, and it is by HIS love for us that HE has corrected our errors of sin by giving us a way out of condemnation to become free from sin and the Second Death of our Spirit so we may return to HIM free of sin and full of the Spirit of enlightenment.

There is no other way except through believing our Lord Jesus Christ without doubt or fear. Following Him by keeping His commands that He teaches us every day is showing that you believe in Him and that you love Him. And our GOD the Father will love you as HIS Child now and forever.

Most people are already keeping some of these commands by common sense in their own nature. They may just need to fine-tune their habits to conform with the rest of the commands to be perfectly good in nature. Of course, we must remember the commands that came from our GOD the Father to keep them by heart. These are HIS Commands that He gave us through our Lord Jesus Christ:

Love GOD with all your heart, mind, and soul.

Love your neighbor.

Honor your mother and father.

Do not commit adultery.

Do not murder.

Do not steal.

Do not bear false witness.

Always love each other as our Lord Jesus Christ loves us. This is the New Command.

There is one more thing that our Lord Jesus Christ teaches us that every Chosen One must learn to become mature in Spirit. I know it has been the catalyst that I needed to master every challenge that I have ever faced and learned from in the Word of Truth. First, I learned to live with no doubt and believe in Him with all my heart, mind, and soul, while living in the Spirit, before I could do what He asks of me; and that is: Do Not Fear.

I am a person born into this world just like anyone else in this realm, only I am a Chosen One who received the Chrism of my Lord Jesus Christ at an early age. I believe it was because of my nature that I did not have the desires in me to do anything to break the commands. I have loved Him unconditionally before I knew all these commands were written for people to learn to keep as adults. Our Lord Jesus Christ sees something good deep inside each of us before we know about it enough in ourselves to decide to live by it. This allows us to become Chosen Ones living in Spirit because it is in our nature. Everyone who is given a message from GOD is surprised in one way or another that they were chosen to do HIS work. And every one of them that believed in the power of GOD lived up to HIS expectations or they would be corrected in their ways of error by HIM.

There has to come a point in time for those who are blessed in this life to realize that all the things that have been given to them have been done to wake them up and compel them to commit themselves to use that goodness that is deep inside themselves to follow the Word of Truth, who is our Lord Jesus Christ, and to help Him bring others to do the same. We must help others to know Him and our GOD the Father to be anointed with the Holy Spirit for eternal life. That is the Chrism of the Child that we as Children in Spirit must receive to mature in Spirit. We came from GOD the Father when we were first created, and we are recreated in Spirit to do HIS will before we return to HIM in perfect Spirit. It's with the Word of Truth that we help feed the hungry to help sanctify their minds, and it's by turning them to our Lord Jesus Christ for the repentance of their sins that the thirst of the thirsty is quenched to sanctify their Body-Temple to become ready to receive the Holy Spirit and the Spirit of our Lord Jesus Christ. It's with the Chrism of the Holy Spirit that their Spirit becomes enlightened by the truth. That is how we become Chosen Ones living in the Spirit who have crossed over from the condemnation of being doomed to death to becoming Resurrected into a Child of GOD living by the Spirit in Complete Unity for eternal life.

We live by understanding that the only religion that is acceptable to our GOD the Father, which is to care for the orphans and the widows who both lack leadership to help them become and stay strong in faith to stay attached to our Lord Jesus Christ. This means helping to raise and care for the weak. We must keep ourselves and help others from becoming condemned by the corruption from the sin of this world that leads to death. As a Chosen One, I am held responsible for the lives of anyone I can help turn to my Lord Jesus Christ for the salvation that can only be given through having Him with themselves as One in Spirit. Everyone must receive Him through having faith and giving from the heart through having the love of our Lord Jesus Christ. Faith is for receiving His love, and His love in us is for giving love to others. Both must be done living in Spirit with Him.

I was not exempt from being tempted to fall into weakness before I sorted out how to learn the commands living in this world and keep them. But I know our Lord Jesus Christ sees our goodness and knows our abilities to become Children of GOD. He has patience with each of us, but we need to know how important it is to act upon the opportunity that He has provided for us while living in this body of flesh before it is too late and we become lost forever by death without receiving the power of His Resurrection in our Body-Temple for eternal life.

Take the example of GOD's patience to forgive from the days of Noah. The people of the world did every vile thing in evil that they could think of, but the patience and mercy of GOD the Father for one hundred and twenty years held a message for them to resist evil and turn back to HIM, and in response to that, He would not send a flood to destroy them.

Without seeking the truth, you cannot find the truth because finding the truth is knowing it is a command for you to find it, then to keep it in your heart, and hidden in your mind for eternal life. Therefore, actively keeping the commands of the truth is having the truth.

VINCENTE GARCIA

A Chosen One must have the Word of Truth written in their heart by keeping the love of the truth hidden in their minds to remember the truth and follow the truth within their Body-Temple while living in the Spirit to prove that they love our Lord Jesus Christ with all their heart, mind, and Spirit.

I have laid down my old life in the flesh to become alive in my new life living in Spirit, being led by the Holy Spirit of my GOD the Father, to help others learn and understand this truth to serve my GOD the Father through my Lord Jesus Christ. Just because I knew my Lord Jesus Christ at a young age did not exempt me from becoming refined through my own trials and tribulations that the Spiritual path of my life brought my way. I had to learn from the Holy Spirit about having a higher level of faith through practicing my faith, self-control, power, and patience.

And I am letting you know this: I could not have lived through all these things that I saw, did, and learned from my Lord Jesus Christ, if I had not first learned with His help to never fear. Fear holds us back from learning the Word of Truth; fear leads to sin; therefore, fear is sin. Learn to never fear, and to always, without fail, trust our Lord Jesus Christ as you pray in Spirit to our GOD the Father without fear or doubt because HE loves you and has already proven it through HIS Son Jesus Christ.

FROM GOD

This is the Word of Truth that our Lord Jesus Christ teaches us, but some people seem not understand this after knowing the bible verses enough to recite them. This is why it's so important to learn the meaning of the commands: do not ever fear our GOD the Father, and always love our GOD the Father with all your heart, mind, and soul.

Here is an example of this truth. Think of a time when you loved someone like your newborn baby, your sibling, mother, father, or best friend, and you could feel that you loved them unconditionally. If you can imagine, with that kind of love, that you are looking at your own baby in your arms, and you know that your baby, who is staring at you, has pure love for you and you have pure love for your baby. Would you have any fear of your own newborn baby that you love? Of course not. You love your baby with every fiber of your body, and you would die fighting for and protecting your baby that you love from anything that is trying to harm your baby. That is what loving with all your heart, mind, and soul truly means, and there is no room for fear -no fear at all when you love someone with all your heart, mind, and soul.

This is why it is so important to learn what is consistent in the teachings of our Lord Jesus Christ when He teaches us to pray in Spirit as we worship our GOD the FATHER because the Chosen Ones are being called to HIM through our Lord Jesus Christ. The hearts of the

VINCENTE GARCIA

Chosen Ones are being searched by our GOD the Father, and He tells us to glorify our GOD the Father in the Name of HIS Son Jesus Christ. That means to ask of HIM in the Name of HIS Son, Jesus Christ, and HE will give you what you ask for if you believe without any doubt that you already have it. That is having the power of faith in GOD through HIS Son Jesus Christ. This is the power of prayer that we are given by being anointed with HIS Holy Spirit. The Word of Truth is you must not fear or doubt when you pray to our GOD the Father through our Lord Jesus Christ in a pure Spirit.

That is why our Lord Jesus Christ said that He will not ask HIM for you, and that you must ask of HIM for yourself on your own by asking of HIM in the Name of His Son Jesus Christ to show HIM that you honor HIS Son, and by that you therefore honor HIM. You must ask HIM yourself because HE loves you.

In our relationship with our GOD the Father, we live for our GOD the Father through our Lord Jesus Christ and with HIS Holy Spirit who is guiding us to all the Word of Truth. He recreated us this way to live eternal life which was HIS intention for us since the first Man HE created. We came from GOD who is love. Living eternal life by the Spirit in Complete Unity, as a Chosen Spiritual One does, leaves no room for fear or doubt where there is only the existence of pure eternal love for each other. This is why our Lord Jesus Christ reiterated many times when He gave us the New Command of the New

Covenant living in Spirit, which is: "Always love each other."

All the things that my GOD the Father has given to me through HIS Son Jesus Christ are from my GOD the Father. And all the things that I have been given as blessings are for me to have a stronger faith in HIM through my Lord Jesus Christ. This testimony of my relationship with them, that I share with others, is to help others believe in them and to know that we came from the only Almighty Living GOD who is our Creator through HIS Son, our Lord Jesus Christ.

Chapter 20 - To God

As a Chosen Spiritual One who is constantly being refined to perfection, I will always contemplate on the Word of Truth to help me understand the deeper meanings of what was said and written in scripture; and what I am directly given to serve the purpose of my life in my service to my GOD the Father through HIS Son my Lord Jesus Christ while I am being led to understand the truth by the Holy Spirit that came out of my GOD the Father and into me. And by everything I have learn from my Lord Jesus Christ, I know that I am living as One in Spirit with them, and I am on my way back to my GOD the Father through my Lord Jesus Christ, who is the one who will take me to HIM. It was my decision to accept HIS gift of Eternal Life and to continue to remain committed to stay on the path that HE has destined for me to follow His Son back to HIM as a pure Child of Light.

This is why it is so important to understand the meaning of the knowledge that I am given in symbols, signs, dreams, sounds, visions, and vibrations that I use all my senses to interpret the truth in those languages. And it is my responsibility to help others learn to do the same. In other words, we all must learn our own testimony of how we have been blessed in our lives by preferably writing them down and keeping an account to remember how our GOD the Father is calling us to

VINCENTE GARCIA

HIM through HIS Son Jesus Christ. And when you are ready, you can share your testimony with others to help them strengthen their faith to know that we are a Holy Family as Children of our GOD the Father and co-heirs with our Lord Jesus Christ.

My Lord Jesus Christ said He was sent by my GOD the Father, that He came from GOD, and that He is returning to our GOD the Father. As a Chosen Spiritual One, those words ring profound throughout my entire being since I am created me again as One in Complete Unity with them without sin or shame. And I will not see judgment when I am raised up to see my Lord Jesus Christ to be presented to my GOD the Father.

My Lord Jesus Christ taught me that there were two things, Water and Spirit, which were at the beginning of creation before the beginning of the creation of the world. We must become water, and Spirit before we can enter the Kingdom of Heaven. Our Body-Temple is with the water and was made alive with a Spirit in our first creation. That Spirit is alone and can be extinguished if it remains that way. We must cross over from that condition which leads to death by receiving the Holy Spirit with our Spirit, and the Spirit of our Lord Jesus Christ, who has the Spirit of GOD the Father to give us eternal life. We must become One Spirit with them to become Water and Spirit with eternal life to enter the Kingdom of Heaven within us as we are in our Body-Temple. That is called the Resurrection, which means we crossed over from death to life. We will live by the will of our GOD the Father on earth as we will in HIS Heavenly Kingdom. The Fire and Light of the Holy Spirit will be with us at the death of our Body-Temple to redeem us and raise us up into a Spirit-Body with eternal life to enter the Spiritual Realm in the eternal Kingdom of GOD the Father in Heaven.

Water has life, like Spirit has life in creation, for that purpose it is for creation from the beginning. And I know that our GOD the Father is Spirit of the Brightest Living Light that hovers above the Water of Life that is with HIM. HE is without beginning or end and was not created; therefore, HE is the power source of all life who was not given a Name, because there was no one else before HIM to Name HIM. HE cannot be limited to any language or name because HE is greater than all thoughts, given words, and names. We use words to describe what we think HE is, but no one can say they know HIS name or form, since HIS form is hidden from us. HE is called the Invisible Living GOD of all creation. And HIS Created Son, who is our Lord Jesus Christ, refers to HIM as His Father and our Father in Heaven because all that is created must worship our Invisible Living GOD through HIS Son.

We should pray silently while giving thanks in pure Spirit, and focus intently in our minds on the One and only true Living GOD and Creator, who created HIS one and only Son, and gave Him a Holy Name of power above all names: Jesus Christ. HE knows that you are asking of HIM through your heart and by the groans of the Holy Spirit that knows you better than yourself. Remember, it is through our Lord Jesus Christ that we are to acknowledge our GOD the Father in this day and age. He is the Word of our GOD the Father and is over all language and all creation that was created through Him by the will of our GOD the Father, which is by the Forethought and Foreknowledge of our GOD the Father, who has given the power of the Spirit for creation of all things to our Lord Jesus Christ. This is how and why He is called the Word, the Anointed One, the Christ, and the only begotten Son of our GOD the Father; and all things were created through Him even before the earth was made.

The only begotten Son was Anointed with powers we call Spirits. And they are Forethought, Foreknowledge, Incorruptibility, Eternal Life, and Truth. And with these Spirit Powers by the will of our GOD the Father, He used them from within Himself and created all creation and all living things in the Heavens and Earth in perfect bodies for the Realm they exist.

When our Lord Jesus Christ created the first man and woman, they were perfectly created in the image of GOD to live eternal in bodies made for Paradise. They communicated directly with the Angels from Heaven who helped care for their Realm in Paradise for them.

There was division between the heavenly beings that fought for the dominion over Humanity due to their jealousy of man and their desire to be worshipped by man as a god, when they themselves should have honored Humanity as a creation made in the Image of GOD the Father. The angel Lucifer, called Satan, also called the Serpent or the Dragon, and the Father of Lies, was leading his following angels and fought with the Angel Michael and his Angels, when Michael and his Angels cast Satan and his following angels out of the heavenly realm and down to Earth until it is their appointed time for their doom and destruction.

The first two created people transgressed against the Word when they ate of the Tree of Knowledge of good and evil, which they were warned not to. They were transformed into bodies of flesh that would die as they were told would happen because of the sin in them that created death of the flesh. The Angels that serve our GOD the Father removed them from the place of Paradise and guarded it so they could not reenter it because if they ate of the Tree of Life in Paradise, they would remain that way. They were sorry for what they did, and our Lord Jesus Christ assured them that there would come a day when a man from the lineage of their offspring would redeem them by correcting this error. Our Lord Jesus Christ made this promise with them and assured them that He would be the man that will redeem humanity. At that time, they were not told how it would be done.

Then there was an Old Covenant made for the people of Israel at Mount Sinai called the Mosaic Law that set forth conditions for them to live by to please our GOD the Father. It was transitory until a superior New Covenant would be made at the appointed time.

When the time was fulfilled and our GOD the Father asked who would be the one to be a redemption for mankind, His only created Son, HIS Christ, our Lord Jesus Christ answered HIM to let HIM know that He was ready to do HIS will to fulfill the promise that He made to the first two humans, as it's written in scripture. This event marked the beginning of the New Covenant of the Spirit to be fulfilled by our Lord Jesus Christ, who would be killed as an innocent man without sin in the flesh on Earth. He is called the Lamb of GOD, because He was the final sacrifice for all sin to be forgiven in anyone of the world that believes in Him, accepts Him, and keeps His commands. And by having His Spirit of Life in Unity we are given eternal life by HIM before our Body-Temple dies.

Here are the relations of how the error of man was corrected by a man of equal nature. The first man was made perfect without a human father and his Spirit was placed into flesh for his flesh to die for the sin in him. My Lord Jesus Christ was created Incorruptible without a human father and His Spirit was placed into flesh from the offspring of the first man, the virgin woman Mary, who was born out of the lineage of the flesh from the first man. And He remained without sin when His Body-Temple of flesh was killed on a crucifix. He voluntarily allowed His innocent body to be subject to death without sin as a Superior sin offering and the final sacrifice of Human Flesh for all sin to be forgiven for all who believe in Him.

Therefore, the power of sin and death no longer has any power to enslave the Children of our GOD the Father in their bodies to keep them falling short of having the glory of eternal life. And so long as we keep the commands given to us by our Lord Jesus Christ and believe in His power of the New Covenant of the Spirit, we can have eternal Life. That is the Testimony of our GOD the Father.

I know that our Lord Jesus Christ did things for us as a symbol for us to remember Him. One thing He told us to do was to eat bread to remember His flesh and drink from the cup of wine to remember His Blood. That is why He preached, unless you eat of my flesh and drink of my blood, you do not have life. Those who do not have an understanding of the truth in the Word did not know the meaning of His statement. These words are symbols to remember to have the Word of Truth and receive the Holy Spirit with repentance.

The bread is the Word of Truth that we follow in Spirit and keep hidden in our minds for our own self-control of our flesh. The cup that we drink from is two parts, with one part water that is to sanctify the water in our Body-Temple as a repentance from sin, and the second part wine is to sanctify the blood in our Body-Temple for receiving His Spirit and the Holy Spirit into our heart, which that makes us perfectly clean in our Body-Temple heart, mind, and soul. This is how we are symbolically receiving the sacrificial flesh, blood, and Spirit of our Lord Jesus Christ. This we do to remember Him for all these things He has done for us, for our sanctification first, and then our salvation by receiving His Spirit, the Fire of Life within Him, and the Chrism of the Holy Spirit from our GOD the Father.

Keep in mind that our Lord Jesus Christ came to this Earthly Realm for the salvation of Adam and his offspring by cleansing all creation of earth and water from the power of sin and death that condemns us. When He received the baptism of John the Baptist, He did not receive the baptism of water to cleanse Himself of sin. He never sinned. When He received the baptism of water, He poured out all the evil and sin in water with His perfect and Holy Body-Temple to sanctify the water of all creation. He did the same for the rest of creation when His Sacred Blood was sacrificed and shed on the Earth to cleanse it when the final sacrifice was completed. The Heavens turned dark like night and opened up at noon to reveal the stars of the sky after He was on the cross for three hours of daylight since nine o'clock in the morning, which was called the third hour of the day. So, He was on the cross for exactly three hours of daylight first and exactly three hours of night darkness until three o'clock in the afternoon, which was called the ninth hour. The Archangel Michael and his Angels came down from Heaven and worshiped Jesus while He was on the cross. As our Lord Jesus Christ committed His Spirit into the hands of our GOD the Father and His Sacred Blood was shed onto the Earth, the Earth shook violently, splitting the rocks and tombs broke open.

Now, there is no more need for sacrifice by the Chosen Ones who receive our Lord Jesus Christ. The Old Covenant had been fulfilled and has been transcended by the New Covenant of the Spirit of our Lord Jesus Christ, which is the Testimony of our GOD the Father concerning His Son Jesus Christ. The Ark of the Covenant was under His Crucifix in the ground and placed there by an Angel sent by GOD in Heaven. The Angel was commanded by GOD the Father to save the things that were in the Holy of Holies, so they would not be taken by the Babylonians. The Angel took everything out of the Temple from the Holy of Holies and then commanded the Earth to open and swallow up all the things that the Angel had placed there in the Earth. This took place just before the destruction of the Holy City and Temple of Solomon in Jerusalem when the Babylonian armies were outside of the walls of the Holy City; and it was the plan of our GOD the Father to allow it to happen before the temple was rebuilt later and called the Temple of Herod when our Lord Jesus Christ was sent to Earth from Heaven by our GOD the Father.

When the Holy Temple was rebuilt by Herod, at the time my Lord Jesus Christ was crucified, the Ark of the Covenant was still hidden from people in the Earth and was not in the Temple of Jerusalem that was rebuilt by Herod and called the Temple of Herod. Therefore, when the Sacred Blood Sacrifice of our Lord Jesus Christ was spilled from His Body-Temple on the Crucifix, His blood ran down the cross and into the rocks in the earth that were split under the cross by earthquakes. And when His Sacred Blood entered into the Earth where the Ark of the Covenant was at that time, it was the fulfillment of the final sprinkling of Blood Sacrifice on the Ark of the Covenant that was at that time below Him in the Earth. And at that very moment, the prophecy of the Old Covenant of the Law was superseded by the Superior New Covenant of the Spirit of our Lord Jesus Christ, ending the Old Covenant Mosaic Law. And so it has come to pass that the Mosaic Old Covenant of the Law, which was first, is now put last; while the Blood Sacrifice of our Lord Jesus Christ and the creation of the New Covenant, which came last, is now put first in superiority. That which is first will be last, and that which is last will be first.

Everything is being turned from death to life with the power of life over death through our Lord Jesus Christ. He was the final Sacrifice of Perfect Human Flesh that changed all creation to become free of sin through Him and for those believing in Him in Spirit. From that time on, there is no need for any more animal sacrifice for those who believe in Him. Because we know that there is no greater Sacrifice than the Human Flesh of our Lord Jesus Christ, the Son of our GOD the Father. And that is what our Lord Jesus Christ meant when He said on the Crucifix, it is done.

No one carries the sin of the first man; he had to pay for that himself. We fall into condemnation by the sin of the flesh on our own. And we must learn, believe, receive, and keep the commands of our GOD the Father in the Name of our Lord Jesus Christ to live in Spirit by the New Covenant of our GOD the Father concerning HIS Son Jesus Christ, who is our Lord, Teacher, and Savior for us to cross over from the status of condemnation of destruction by the Second Death of our Spirit in the Lake of Fire, to the status of eternal life of our Resurrected Spirit to have eternal life in the Kingdom of GOD.

When we live in the Spirit, we pray to ask of our GOD the Father in the Name of our Lord Jesus Christ to forgive us of our sin for repentance, as we are also asking our Lord Jesus Christ in His Name to be with us in Spirit Complete Unity as we vow to keep His commands. Then we ask HIM in the Name of HIS Son Jesus Christ to send us HIS Holy Spirit out from HIM and into us to guide us. The same is true that if you ask our Lord Jesus

Christ to anoint you with the Holy Spirit of our GOD the Father, He will do it to glorify our GOD the Father.

To remain attached to our Lord Jesus Christ, which is to know Him and our GOD the Father, there are certain things we must do to remember the purpose of our eternal life. First, we must contemplate His Word of Truth. And that is why I was inspired by the Holy Spirit to author a book in Spirit prayer for over a year that is Titled, "Inspiration For Your Eternal Life" and the tag line is Fifteen Ways To Be Saved, because there are fifteen chapters with scripture, a foundational explanation of the Word of Truth, and a prayer at the end of each chapter to help Chosen Spiritual Ones to pray for the things they learn from it.

Remember this, you do not need to know the whole bible to be saved. You only need to know enough to keep His commands and believe in the Testimony of our GOD the Father to accept our Lord Jesus Christ into your heart, mind, and soul to live in Complete Unity. Then live alive in Spirit by the Resurrection and Chrism as a Child of Light now and after our Redemption to eternal life in the Kingdom of GOD.

Some of the things I learned as a Chosen One that helps me quickly remember my purpose are to remember what time it is in this Realm. Today's date is after the Old Covenant has been fulfilled, and I am living in the New Covenant of the Spirit of my Lord Jesus

Christ that I believe in and everything it stands for with all my heart, mind, and soul, living in the Spirit.

When I think back to that time, first, I see the symbol of the cross that is burned into my memory to remind me that my Lord Jesus Christ has already sacrificed Himself for me and all humanity from the first man Adam. I have the symbol of the Cross.

Second, I remember the promise my Lord Jesus Christ made to us was to ask our GOD the Father to send HIS Holy Spirit to help all the Chosen Ones that believe in Him and keep His commands. I live in the Spirit with the Spirit of my Lord Jesus Christ with the Holy Spirit, and I can ask for His help to guide me to any truth I need to know. I have the Holy Spirit.

Third, I have become enlightened by a brighter light of understanding the knowledge I have learned in the Word of Truth that lets me see through the darkness of this Earthly Realm to help others find their way to the Living Light of my Lord Jesus Christ for eternal life. I have the Light of Enlightenment.

Fourthly, I believe in the Resurrection of my Lord Jesus Christ and in my Lord, Teacher, and Savior by accepting Him into my heart, mind, and Spiritual Complete Unity. I have crossed over from death to eternal life, and I have been Resurrected as I have become One with my Lord Jesus Christ in my Body-Temple. I am living in this

Earthly Realm waiting to be Redeemed and transformed into a Spirit-Body in the Realm of the Spirit with the Holy Spirit of our GOD the Father. The Holy Spirit was sent from HIM into me as a deposit and promise now, for me to be resurrected now, and later to be redeemed, transformed into an eternal Spirit of Light with Him at the end of my life here on Earth. I will instantly appear in the Heavenly Realm together with Him to be presented to my GOD the Father. I have the Resurrection with the Holy Spirit. So, I have the Holy Spirit, the Light of Enlightenment, the Cross, and the Resurrection with the Spirit of my Lord Jesus Christ.

Receiving the Holy Spirit is the Chrism of the Chosen One, and I do not doubt that everyone is unique by how they get to a point in their life to become anointed by our Lord Jesus Christ to receive the Holy Spirit and the Spirit of our Lord Jesus Christ for eternal life. If you have read the scriptures of the New Testament, you might remember how our Lord Jesus Christ was on the crucifix and there was another person who was on a crucifix next to Him who saw what had taken place as he confessed that he believed that our Lord Jesus Christ was innocent and is the Son of our GOD the Father. And he asked Him to remember him when He gets to His Kingdom, and our Lord Jesus Christ replied that he would be with Him in paradise that day.

And there is the Book of Revelations that tells of two witnesses that will come from heaven and go to war with the Anti-Christ in Jerusalem in the end times. The Gospel of Nicodemus names the two witnesses as Elijah and Enoch. And it also names a third person named Dimas who was taken up to heaven from the crucifix with the sign of the cross on both of his shoulders. He admitted that he was a thief and committed many kinds of wickedness on earth, but when he saw the amazing signs in creation happening before his eyes, he believed in our Lord Jesus Christ and asked Him to remember him from heaven. These three men were never chained in the darkness of Hell. The Hell that our Lord Jesus Christ made powerless over humanity when He shed His Blood to cleanse the world from sin and He was given the authority over all Heaven, Earth, and Under Earth.

And the final destruction of all evil, death, and Hell will be thrown into what is called the Lake of Fire, which will be the end of all wickedness and non-believers that reject the Word of Truth. That is the Second Death for the condemned, which is the death of their Spirit. From that day forward, death will be nonexistent, the Earth and sky as we know it will also pass away from creation as it cracks apart from the intense heat after the sky is taken away. There will be nothing left of anything that sin had dwelled in, and the remaining life will be perfect as our GOD the Father always intended for HIS creation to live in since before the beginning of creation.

VINCENTE GARCIA

The Chosen Spiritual Ones will not see judgement or be put to shame for condemnation, because we die and are resurrected as a new creation in our Body-Temple now at the time we receive our Lord Jesus Christ with the Holy Spirit in us as One in Complete Unity, like our Lord Jesus Christ was resurrected and recreated by the Holy Spirit of our GOD the Father. We will be transformed into imperishable bodies of Spirit and Water as we are redeemed to a higher state of grace with incorruptibility to live in the New Kingdom, on a New Earth conjoined with a New Heaven with our GOD the Father. We will live with our loved ones who come out from this Earth to our GOD the Father in paradise. And HE will live among us there to be our GOD in Complete Unity, as we live to praise HIM with love for each other forever.

These are the messages that I was given directly from my Lord Jesus Christ: The messages that I had to experience throughout my lifetime were for me to understand the Chrism of the Child that He put in me. I learned that I am recreated me in Spirit, to become perfect in Spirit, so that I may help enlighten His Chosen Ones in the world to know the truth in the Word of GOD by HIS Testimony concerning HIS Son, who is my Lord Jesus Christ. He will bring us all to our GOD the Father in the heavenly realms.

And since HIS will has become my will through my Lord Jesus Christ, it is being done. Until our last day, for those who are saved on earth, the Spirit of the Word lives with us. He is truly our Lord and Savior for all who believe in Him and call on Him by His Name: Jesus Christ of Nazareth- Redemption, by the Way of His Chrism, leads to the Truth; to give us Life. This is the truth in HIS Name and His Chrism of the Child that helps us return to our GOD the Father.

About the Author

Vincente R. Garcia was born in November 1961 in Pontiac, Michigan, and raised in Southern California. About the age of five, he heard the voice of the Lord Jesus Christ, and by the age of seven, he had several spiritual interventions that would set the tone throughout his life. By the age of nine, he would put on a suit and walk alone to the local churches in Torrance, California, to join in singing and praising God in the early Sunday services.

From those early years, he felt a strong connection with the Spirit of our Lord Jesus Christ and knew that he was being called to know Him throughout his life. His focus was to venture on a quest to understand the messages he was shown by searching the Bibles, the KJV, NIV, NWT, Gideon, and Quran, mostly to learn the reason why spirits intervene with humanity and more with some than others.

After high school, he served in the United States Air Force Europe, then served in civil law enforcement in

ABOUT THE AUTHOR

the California Department of Corrections, during which time he also became an Ordained Minister by the Universal Life Church Ministries in June 2022.

Shortly after, in February 2023, he was given a sign that it was time to Minister to the Lord. Without delay, in March 2023, he retired from employment and was immediately guided into powerful Spiritual Prayers for over 12 months, day and night, to write fifteen letters as a foundation of truth for the children in the world that are being called to the living God. These letters are the results of his mission for the chosen ones, to help them understand how to become inspired for eternal life in his first book with bible references, INSPIRATION FOR YOUR ETERNAL LIFE.

His next mission of inspiration led him to write his own journey of the divine interventions throughout his life in CHRISM OF THE CHILD. This explains the mysteries of his spiritual refinement that strengthened his relationship with GOD and HIS Son, our Lord Jesus Christ, and the Holy Spirit that is sent from out of GOD and into HIS chosen ones. It is written for those who have inspiration for eternal life, so they may have insight into what to pay attention to as they are led to the truth by the Holy Spirit to remain in the Chrism of our Lord Jesus Christ without fear or doubt as they honor our Living GOD. This journey will never end.

www.ingramcontent.com/pod-product-compliance
Lightning Source LLC
Chambersburg PA
CBHW050135170426
43197CB00011B/1851